NUMISMATIC STUDIES

No. 16

ALEXANDER'S DRACHM MINTS

I: SARDES AND MILETUS

BY

MARGARET THOMPSON

NUMISMATIC STUDIES
No. 16

THE AMERICAN NUMISMATIC SOCIETY
NEW YORK
1983

ISSN 0517-404x
ISBN 0-89722-193-1

PRINTED IN BELGIUM AT CULTURA, WETTEREN

TABLE OF CONTENTS

FOREWORD

In 1955 Alfred R. Bellinger and the author published a collection of drachms, mainly issues of Alexander the Great and the Diadochi, which had been found at or near Bab some ten years earlier and subsequently acquired by Yale University.[1] Although the hoard was incomplete and not in itself of any great significance, its evidence in combination with that of a number of other hoards laid the groundwork for a synoptic outline of the activity of a group of Asia Minor mints whose output was chiefly small silver. From the beginning it was the authors' intent eventually to expand the condensed conspectuses of the original publication into die studies of the individual mints with proper catalogues and adequate illustration. It is deeply to be regretted that the first and second stages of the project have been separated by so long an interval that the present studies have not had the benefit of Alfred Bellinger's collaboration.[2]

Additional material and research have modified to some extent the initial outline, altering the proposed sequence and chronology at several mints, but the basic structure stands. Under Alexander and the Successors down to the end of the fourth century, seven mints in Asia Minor produced the small change of the entire empire, their very substantial emissions of drachms supplemented at times by much smaller issues of tetradrachms. This pattern is in sharp contrast to that prevailing elsewhere. At all other mints the principal denomination was the tetradrachm; drachms were rarely struck and then only in minor quantity. The reasons for this distinction in the kind of money produced by various mints are no more evident now than they were in 1955. As a regional distinction it conforms to the traditions of the pre-Alexandrine period when the basic unit of exchange for much of Asia Minor was a small silver coin, the Persian siglos or the autonomous drachm, while Macedonia, Cilicia and lands further south and east relied on a large silver coin, the tetradrachm or the shekel. Whether the pattern was set by royal decree or by local authority is a question that cannot be definitively answered but the fact that it endured well after Alexander's death attests its efficacy.

[1] M. Thompson and A. R. Bellinger, "Greek Coins in the Yale Collection, IV: A Hoard of Alexander Drachms," *Yale Classical Studies* 14 (1955), pp. 3-45.

[2] Much of the preliminary work on the drachm mints of Alexander was accomplished during three leaves of absence from the American Numismatic Society: a stay in Copenhagen in 1963, as the guest of the Royal Coin Cabinet and with the aid of a travel grant from the American Council of Learned Societies; a term in 1969 at the Institute for Advanced Study in Princeton; and an appointment as Regents' Professor at the University of California, Berkeley, for the autumn of 1974. I am deeply grateful to all concerned for these research opportunities. I am also indebted to the many colleagues here and abroad who have provided data on specific coins and hoards, and especially to Otto Mørkholm, who has kindly read sections of this manuscript and offered helpful comments. The plates attest the skill of Michael Di Biase and Robert J. Myers.

In addition to small silver, the seven mints produced a surprisingly extensive gold coinage: staters of Alexander and Philip III and posthumous issues of Philip II. The figures are truly impressive. Lampsacus, for example, used over 100 obverse dies for her gold emissions, a total which far surpasses that of the average tetradrachm mint and approaches or even slightly exceeds the output of such major workshops as Amphipolis and Babylon. When the final tally is available, we may find that most of the gold coinage of 330-300 B.C. came from Asia Minor.

The drachm mints under present discussion have been identified as Lampsacus, Abydus, Sardes, Colophon, Magnesia, Miletus and probably Teos. In general the attributions are those of Edward T. Newell but his trays and notes rarely offer any clue as to the basis of his judgment. As is true of the bulk of Alexander's coinage, the earlier Asia Minor issues employ symbols and monograms which are moneyers' marks without civic connotation. They may serve to bring together separate strikings but they are of no real help in determining the location of the mint. Toward the end of the century the situation changes. Lysimachus gains control of northwestern Asia Minor and of the mints which had been coining for Antigonus. As one would logically expect, he keeps them in operation for the production of his own money. Often the same symbols and monograms carry over from Antigonus's final issues to the Alexandrine coins of Lysimachus and then to the latter's own regnal strikings. Some of these symbols now have civic significance and thus confirm the attribution of the series as a whole. Not all mints can be located with the same degree of certainty, but there is more evidence for attribution than might appear at first glance.

Although all seven mints adhere to the basic pattern of monetary production, there are noteworthy variations in the type and quantity of coinage put out and in the chronological span of minting activity. The picture as a whole, however, can best be summarized after the record of the individual mints has been presented. This will be done in three stages. Lampsacus and Abydus are linked in terms of geography and to some extent of style, while the three Ionian mints have elements in common which make it sensible to treat them as a group. Miletus and Sardes are more or less disparate workshops, combined here for the sake of convenience. They have been chosen to initiate the sequence, not because they are the most important of the mints but because their chronologies are comparatively tight and their coinages have a number of unusual features.

In this volume and the one to follow on Lampsacus and Abydus, the primary intent is to present the numismatic evidence without detailed reference to the history of the period. A final section of the third volume, dealing with the Ionian mints, will attempt to analyze the record as a whole in the light of what we know from other sources about events in Asia Minor c. 330-300 B.C.

Throughout the catalogues it is to be understood that the coins, unless otherwise indicated, are the standard gold, silver and bronze types issued in the names of Philip II, Alexander III or IV and Philip III. This is not a corpus in the sense that all available public and private collections have been culled for material; the numerous coins, casts and photo file cards at the ANS provide adequate evidence for the chronological sequence and the relative size of the individual issues. That the record is incomplete with respect to the drachms is clear from the fact that so many die combinations are known from only one example. Obviously a great many more drachm dies were originally employed but even prolonged search is unlikely to give the full story. While the reverses of the gold and the tetradrachms, as well as the smaller drachm issues, have been checked for die-linkage to establish the sequence of emission, only cursory attention has been paid to reverse transfers within the large drachm issues since ascertaining the exact order in which the obverse dies were used does not seem worth the labor involved. Illustration (as indicated by asterisks before catalogue entries) is also less comprehensive for the drachms than for other sections of the coinage. All recorded gold and tetradrachm obverses are shown on the plates but in some instances drachm dies have not been reproduced if they are similar in style to illustrated examples. The numerous hoards, cited parenthetically after individual entries, are identified and discussed in the section on Hoards which concludes the study.

ABBREVIATIONS

Coin Hoards	M. J. Price and D. Nash, eds., *Coin Hoards* (London, 1975-).
Delepierre	A collection in the Paris cabinet in process of publication.
Demanhur	E. T. Newell, *Alexander Hoards, II : Demanhur 1905*, ANSNNM 19 (New York, 1923).
Demetrius	E. T. Newell, *The Coinages of Demetrius Poliorcetes* (London, 1926).
Grose	S. W. Grose, *Catalogue of the McClean Collection of Greek Coins*, 3 vols. (Cambridge, 1923-29).
de Hirsch	P. Naster, *La collection Lucien de Hirsch* (Brussels, 1959)
Hunt.	G. Macdonald, *Catalogue of Greek Coins in the Hunterian Collection* (Glasgow, 1899-1905)
IGCH	M. Thompson, O. Mørkholm, C. M. Kraay, eds., *An Inventory of Greek Coin Hoards* (New York, 1973)
de Luynes	J. Babelon, *Catalogue de la collection de Luynes*, 4 vols. (Paris, 1924-36)
Philippe	G. Le Rider, *Le monnayage d'argent et d'or de Philippe II* (Paris, 1977)
Ptolemies	J. N. Svoronos, *Ta nomismata tou kratous ton Ptolemaion*, 4 vols. (Athens, 1904-8)
Reattrib.	E. T. Newell, *Reattribution of Certain Tetradrachms of Alexander the Great* (New York, 1912)
Sidon and Ake	E. T. Newell, *The Dated Alexander Coinage of Sidon and Ake* (New Haven, 1916)
SNG	*Sylloge Nummorum Graecorum*
Tarsos	E. T. Newell, *Tarsos under Alexander* (New York, 1919)
Weber	L. Forrer, *Descriptive Catalogue of the Collection of Greek Coins Formed by Sir Hermann Weber* (London, 1922-29)
WSM	E. T. Newell, *The Coinage of the Western Seleucid Mints*, ANSNS 4 (New York, 1941)

SARDES

ATTRIBUTION

In his publication of the Demanhur Hoard, Newell assigns three tetradrachms to Sardes: coins with bucranium, Mithras head-trisceles, and [monogram] monogram.[3] His tickets consistently carry the same mint attributions for staters, tetradrachms and drachms of our Series VIII-XXIII. The gold staters of the first six series in the present catalogue were not labelled by Newell but he had placed them in proximity to the Sardes material in his trays and it is evident that he sensed a relationship. Since the six issues are intimately die-linked, they are obviously the output of a single mint. That they are to be associated with the tetradrachms of Demanhur is indicated by one common symbol, the bucranium, and by the close stylistic affinity of some stater and drachm dies with those of the Mithras head emission. Subsequent issues with their extensive die-linkage, combined with the repetition of monograms and symbols, are unquestionably a unified sequence.

Newell, again in *Demanhur*,[4] gives three reasons for his attribution of the tetradrachms to Sardes: the style which points to a mint north and west of the Taurus, the adjustment of dies which characterizes Persian but not Macedonian coinage and hence indicates an eastern mint, and the strong probability that the Persian capital with its active royal mint would have continued to function under Alexander.

Of the three arguments, the last seems the most cogent. The stylistic criterion merely places the coinage in Asia Minor but not necessarily at Sardes and the alignment of dies is no more pronounced in the case of Sardes than in that of other Asia Minor mints. Like the early tetradrachms, the gold and the small silver coins are predominantly adjusted in the 12 o'clock position[5] but there are a fair number of exceptions. The present catalogue records 44 examples of a 6 o'clock relationship, and 40 in which the alignment is at 3 or 9 o'clock. In a few instances divergent relationships appear with coins from the same pair of dies.[6]

Newell's belief that Sardes would have continued to operate under Alexander is surely valid. It was there that darics and sigloi were produced during the period of Persian control and when the city surrendered peacefully in 334 B.C., Alexander came

[3] *Demanhur* 1748-50; nos. 38, 46 and 53 in the catalogue that follows.

[4] Pp. 87-88.

[5] Minor deviation in the direction of 11 or 1 o'clock has been disregarded. As W. P. Wallace points out (*The Euboian League and Its Coinage* [New York, 1956], pp. 89-90) when an obverse head is involved, one does not know what the fixed point may have been: center of the neck, nape or throat.

[6] As for example nos. 3b and 33.

into possession not only of a minting establishment with ample facilities and skilled workmen but also, one assumes, of a goodly supply of Persian bullion. When the time came, a few years later, to add Asia Minor mints to those further south and east which were already striking royal money, it would be surprising indeed if Sardes were not among them.

Of the seven mints responsible for the production of most of the drachm coinage of the empire, the sequences of Miletus, Lampsacus and Magnesia can be identified with certainty or a high degree of probability. The attribution of other discrete series to Abydus, Colophon and Teos is supported by various considerations of style, mint organization and transferred dies, linking them with the output of Lampsacus and Magnesia. One major sequence remains and it is this which is here assigned to Sardes.

CATALOGUE AND COMMENTARIES

Series I. Control: RAM'S HEAD

Staters

Rev. to l., ram's head

1. *Rev.* below wing l., ram's head. *L. Naville Coll.; London; ANS (*SNGBerry* 164), 8.55↑
2. *L. Naville Coll.[7] With shell added to die below ram's head: *ANS (Asia Minor '50), 8.63↑

Series II. Control: STAG'S HEAD

Staters

Rev. to l., stag's head

3. *Obv.* of 1.
   a. *ANS (Asia Minor '50), 8.51↓; Milan; Hermitage, 8.52↓; London; L. Naville Coll.; Coin Galleries Apr. 20, 1961, 5 (= Coin Galleries FPL 4, Sept. 1960, G369 = Asia Minor '50)
   b. Berlin (Larnaca); ANS (Asia Minor '50), 8.60↓; Helbing Nov. 8, 1928, 3834 (= Weber 2078 = Naville 5, June 18, 1923, 1393), 8.59↑
4. *Obv.* of 2. *Rev.* of 3b. *ANS, 8.48↑
5. *Rev.* of 3b. *L. Naville Coll.; London; Paris (Delepierre 974); ANS (*SNGBerry* 165 = Asia Minor, '50), 8.60↓

[7] M. Naville confirmed in correspondence that his coin showed no trace of the shell which is clear on the ANS piece.

Series III. Control: SERPENT

Staters

Rev. to l., serpent

6. *Obv.* of 5. *ANS, 8.54↑
7a. *Rev.* of 6. *Copenhagen (*SNG* 649), 8.57↑
b. Commerce (No. Greece '66), 8.57
8. *Ives Coll.; London; Florence; Coin Galleries May 24, 1972, 2, 8.63
9a. *Rev.* of 8. ANS. 8.50↓; Hermitage (Anadol), 8.46↓; Commerce (No. Greece '66), 8.57; Sotheby June 2, 1924, 287
b. *London
10. *Stack's ANA Conv. Aug. 10, 1971, 1486, 8.59; Stack's Oct. 1960, 85
11a. *Rev.* of 10. ANS cast (Topolovo)
b. *Commerce (No. Greece '66), 8.57
c. Burgas (Jasna Poljana)
12a. *Rev.* of 11c. The Hague; ANS (*SNGBerry* 166), 8.60↑; Commerce 1922
b. *Paris; Burgas (Jasna Poljana)
13. *Rev.* of 12b. *London
14. *Commerce (Asia Minor '64)
15. *Berlin, 8.62↓

Series IV. Control: GRIFFIN'S HEAD

Staters

Rev. to l., griffin's head

16. *Obv.* of 7. *ANS, 8.55↑; Commerce 1937, 8.57
17. *Hermitage (= Schlessinger Feb. 4, 1935, 656), 8.63↑
18. *Obv.* of 14.
a. *Rev.* of 16. Brussels (de Hirsch 1050), 8.56↑
b. *ANS, 8.56↑
19. *Obv.* of 15.
a. Copenhagen cast (Young Coll.)
b. *Paris
20. *Rev.* of 19b. *Vienna; London (Larnaca); Vinchon Nov. 24, 1969, 8.57
21a. *Rev.* of 18b. Commerce (Paeonia), 8.58↑
b. *Rev.* of 19b. *Saroglos Coll.
22. *Naville 6, Jan. 28, 1924, 708 (= Sotheby May 4, 1908, 304), 8.56; Hermitage, 8.55↑; Lanz Dec. 8, 1972, 72, 8.57

Half Staters

Rev. as above

23. *Glendining Feb. 12, 1958, 1343 (= Naville 17, Oct. 3, 1934, 371 = Naville 1, Apr. 4, 1921, 875 = Egger Nov. 28, 1904, 588), 4.29; London; Münz. u Med. FPL 200, May 1960, 4, 4.13

Quarter Staters

Rev. as above

24. *Paris, 2.16↑; Glasgow (Hunt. 1, p. 299, 36), 2.14

Drachms

Rev. as above

25. *Hersh Coll. (Asia Minor '64), 4.37↑; Saroglos Coll.

Series V. Control: TRIPOD

Staters

Rev. to l., tripod

26. *Obv.* of 14. *ANS, 8.55↑
27. *Obv.* of 20.
   a. *Rev.* of 26. *ANS, 8.57↓
   b. Coin Galleries FPL 6, 1962, F5
28. *Obv.* of 21. *Rev.* of 27b. *Vienna; London
29. *Obv.* of 9. *Rev.* of 27b. *ANS, 8.49↑
30. *Obv.* of 15. *Copenhagen (*SNG* 645), 8.62↑; Commerce (Paeonia), 8.55

Quarter Staters

Rev. as above

31. *Obv.* of 24. *Münz. u. Med. Dec. 2, 1975, 73 (= Münz. u. Med. FPL 247, Sept. 1964, 11 = Asia Minor '64), 2.14; Glendining Oct. 4, 1957, 53, 2.14
32. *Rev.* of 31. *Paris, 2.16↑

Series VI. Control: BUCRANIUM

Staters

Rev. to l., bucranium

33. *Obv.* of 15. *ANS (Saida?), 8.52↑; Cambridge (*SNGLewis* 502), 8.63↑; Commerce (No. Greece '66), 8.59; Sotheby Sept. 28, 1973, 12, 8.54; with reverse die recut: ANS, 8.61↓
34. *Obv.* of 13. *London; L. Naville Coll.; Commerce 1929, 8.52↓
35. *Obv.* of 12.
   a. *Rev.* of 34. Burgas (Jasna Poljana)
   b. *Saroglos Coll.; Commerce (No. Greece '66), 8.54
36. *Rev.* of 35b. *ANS, 8.57↑
37a. *Hermitage, 8.56↑; Grabow July 9, 1930, 286, 8.57; Commerce (Asia Minor '64)
   b. Bourgey June 17, 1974, 6, 8.60

Tetradrachm

Rev. as above

38. *ANS (Demanhur; *Reattrib.*, pl. 17, 1), 17.20↑

Drachms

Rev. as above

39. *ANS (Armenak), 4.11↑; Hersh Coll. (Asia Minor '64), 4.32↑

Series VII. Control: CANTHARUS

Drachms

Rev. to l., cantharus

40. *Egger May 2, 1912, 744
41. *ANS (*SNGBerry* 257), 4.27↑
42a. *ANS (Sinan), 4.24↑; London
b. ANS, 3.98↑
c. ANS (Sinan), 4.25↑
43. *ANS (Sinan), 4.22↑; Hermitage

Series VIII. Control: MITHRAS HEAD

Staters

Rev. to l., Mithras head

44. *ANS, 8.59↓
45. *London; Berlin, 8.55↑

Tetradrachms

Rev. to l., Mithreas head; below throne, trisceles

46. *ANS (Demanhur; Sotheby Apr. 30, 1958, 55), 17.23↑; London, 17.14↑

Drachms

Rev. to l., Mithras head

47. *Obv.* of 43. *ANS, 4.00↑
48. *London
49. *Athens

Bronze Units

Rev. below club, trisceles

50. *ANS, 5.42←
51. *London

Series I-VI form a compact group of issues, linked by a complicated pattern of transferred dies. Output is almost exclusively gold staters, supplemented by some fractional gold, as well as a few tetradrachms and drachms. It is the staters that provide the basic evidence for the sequence or contemporaneity of issues, which may be outlined as follows:[8]

Ram's head	*Stag's head*	*Serpent*	*Griffin's head*	*Tripod*	*Bucranium*
1.———	3.				
2.———	4.				
	5.———	6.			
		7.———	16.		
		14.———	18.———	26.	
		15.———	19.———	30.———	33.
		9.———	———	29.	
		12.———	———	———	35.
		13.———	———	———	34.
			20.———	27.	
			21.———	28.	
			24.———	31.	

Clearly some at least of the symbols must have been employed concurrently. The striking with ram's head has been placed first since one of its reverse dies has the symbol below Nike's wing; thereafter the symbol is centered in the left field. Two obverse dies link Series I and II; there is one link between Series II and III. Thus far there seems to be an orderly progression of emissions with output on a modest scale.

From that point on, the picture changes. The serpent issue uses ten obverse dies, of which one is a carry-over. Six of the remaining nine are shared with other issues. Of the nine obverse dies of the griffin's head striking, three for staters and one for quarters are shared; all seven dies employed with tripod reverses are used for other issues with the exception of one quarter-stater obverse; the bucranium issue shows a transfer of three of its five obverses. Noteworthy is the linkage of serpent, griffin's head, tripod and bucranium (nos. 15, 19, 30, 33). If we had, however, a full record of the original coinage, this might not be an isolated example of multiple transfer.

In all probability, the issues with griffin's head, tripod and bucranium—and possibly with serpent as well—were in simultaneous production, obverse dies being shifted at random among the various anvils. If this is true, it indicates a brief period of concentrated coinage. How brief is a difficult question. Only eighteen obverse dies for staters plus three for fractional gold are catalogued. It is unlikely that minting extended over more than three years; the time span may have been even shorter.

In view of the foregoing, it is obvious that the sequence of issues as outlined in the catalogue is to some extent arbitrary. Ram's head, stag's head and serpent are surely

[8] The numbers are those of the catalogue entries.

the earliest strikings, with some degree of concurrent production a possibility. At the other end, the bucranium issue in its introduction of the tetradrachm denomination and in the style of its one drachm obverse seems to foreshadow the cantharus and Mithras head emissions. There is no evidence for the relative position of the griffin's head and tripod issues; they may have appeared in reverse order or simultaneously.

At least two hands are apparent in the obverse dies. Style 1, characterized for the most part by corkscrew locks of hair and by an upswept helmet-crest terminal ( ), is dominant in the early stage of the coinage and recurs sporadically thereafter.[9] With Style 2 the hair is generally loose and the triple strands of the crest fold in toward Athena's neck ()[10]. Dies such as 12, 13 and 22 may be variants of Style 2 or the work of still a third engraver.

One anomaly among the early stater dies is found in the Mithras head issue. No. 45 is in the standard Sardian tradition; no. 44 is not only alien in style but strikingly similar to some dies at Miletus. Compare, for example, Plate 2, 44 and Plate 21, 8. Either this is an instance of truly expert imitation or, as seems more likely, the Milesian die-cutter was trained at Sardes and then went south to work for the Carian mint.

A single pair of drachm dies is known for the griffin's head issue and another singleton for the bucranium. After that, drachms are produced regularly and provide the link (nos. 43 and 47) between the cantharus and Mithras head issues.[11] The former is represented only by drachms but it may originally have had large silver and even gold. During this early period tetradrachms are exceedingly rare; one specimen of no. 38 and two of no. 46 are the extent of the present record.

The symbols for the most part are banal representations which are of no help in identifying the minting city. The one exception is the Mithras head of Series VIII, an appropriate emblem for a former Persian capital. Otherwise the controls belong to the common repertoire of symbols employed on the Alexander coinage as a whole. In themselves they are by no means exclusively Sardian and therein lies the possibility of misattribution. A ram's head, both below the wing of Nike and in the left field, occurs at Salamis in combination with obverses of quite different style from those of Sardes.[12] Another ram's head in the left field is part of the Magnesian sequence,[13] its provenance attested by the tiny ram's head below the neck of Athena which marks the early output of that Ionian mint. A small stag's head below Nike's wing is found on coins of Teos, with the obverse crest terminals taking the form of a fulmen as they do on other specimens with a griffin below the wing. On these issues as on the coins with griffin, one of which was erroneously attributed to Sardes in *SNGBerry* (no. 167), Nike is advancing in contrast to the static pose of the early Sardian issues. The cantharus, too, is an ambivalent symbol, appearing at Tarsus as well as Amphipolis.[14] Only the Mithras head is found at Sardes alone.

[9] As Plate 1, 1-8.

[10] As Plate 1, 9 and 19–21.

[11] Note also the close stylistic similarity of the bucranium obverse (no. 39).

[12] E. T. Newell, in his notebooks, assigns the coins to Salamis.

[13] A specimen from the Jasna Poljana Hoard is illustrated on Plate 33, 19.

[14] Newell, *Tarsos*, pp. 23-24. For Amphipolis, see Plate 33, 13.

Series IX. Control: [monogram]

Stater

Rev. to r., [monogram]

52. *Rev.* to l., rose (?) erased from die. *ANS, 8.46↑

Tetradrachm

Rev. below throne, [monogram] and dot above strut

53. *ANS (Demanhur; *Reattrib.*, pl. 16, 12), 17.14↑

Drachms

Rev. to l., [monogram]; below, rose

54a. *Rev.* to l., rose; below, [monogram] and dot above strut. *ANS (Sinan), 4.20↑
b. *Rev.* to l., rose; below, ·[monogram]. London; Berry Coll., 4.16; Schlessinger Feb. 4, 1935, 715, 4.20
c. *ANS (Sinan), 4.23↑
55. Benson Coll., 4.19↑; Athens (Corinth), 4.10
56a. *ANS (Sinan), 4.22↑
b. ANS (Sinan), 4.19↑
57a. *ANS (Sinan), 4.26↑
b. *Rev.* of 56b. ANS (Sinan), 4.25↑
c. Cambridge (*SNGLeake* 2233), 4.05↑
d. Turin, 4.09↑
58a. *ANS (Sinan), 4.24→
b. ANS (Sinan), 4.26↑; ANS, 4.13↑
c. ANS (Sinan), 3.78↑
d. Hersh Coll. (Asia Minor '64), 4.26↑
59a. *ANS (Sinan), 4.29↑; ANS (Sinan), 4.16↑
b. ANS (Sinan), 4.09↑
60a. *ANS (Sinan), 4.27↑
b. ANS (Sinan), 4.24↑
c. ANS, 4.19↑
61a. *ANS (Cavalla), 4.13↑
b. ANS (Sinan), 4.29↑
62. *ANS (Cavalla), 4.08↑
63a. ANS, 3.67↑
b. ANS, 3.99↑
c. Hermitage
64. *Hermitage

Rev. to l., [monogram]; to r., club

65a. *ANS (Larissa), 4.10↑; ANS, 4.10↑
b. ANS, 4.21↑

66a. *ANS (Larissa), 4.16↑
b. ANS (Sinan), 4.09↑
c. ANS (Armenak), 4.16↑
d. ANS (Sinan), 4.22↑
67a. *ANS (Larissa), 4.16↑; ANS (Sinan), 4.12↑; Hermitage
b. ANS (Armenak), 4.09↑
c. ANS (Sinan), 4.25↑
d. Cambridge (*SNGLeake* 2232), 4.10↑
68a. *ANS, 4.21↑; Glasgow (Hunt. 1, p. 319, 212), 4.19
b. London
c. Rauch June 4, 1971, 34, 3.80
69. ANS (Sinan), 4.24↑
70. *Rev.* of 69. *ANS (Sinan), 4.24↑
71. *ANS (Cavalla), 4.24↑
72. *The Hague; Oxford (*SNG* 2830), 3.83↑

Bronze Units

Rev. below club, [monogram]

73. *ANS, 6.09↑
74. *ANS, 6.38↓
74a. *ANS, 6.72←

With Series IX the mint begins a large-scale production of drachms and adopts a more elaborate control system. In addition to the monogram, which appears on all strikings, the reverses of the small silver have a secondary control: a rose below Zeus's stool or a club in the outer right field.[15] Obverse dies were apparently not shared between the two symbols.

While the Heracles heads of the silver and bronze of this issue are similar in style to those immediately preceding, the one stater of Series IX is peculiar in several respects. Its obverse die bears no resemblance to any other in either the Sardian sequence or elsewhere in the Alexander coinage. One is tempted to regard it with suspicion but it certainly seems to be genuine,[16] and the deletion of the symbol from the original die is more likely to have happened at the mint than in a forger's workshop. The position of the inscription, reading upward in circular fashion from lower left, is also unparalleled at Sardes although it does occur briefly at Miletus and a few other mints.[17]

[15] This is usually represented with the head up, occasionally with the head down. That the divergent renderings have no significance is evident from the fact that reverses of nos. 66 and 68 show both positions.

[16] Newell, who purchased the coin, had no doubt of its authenticity and several other numismatists who have looked at it concur in his judgment.

[17] Plate 21, 19-21 and Plate 24, 124-27. See also Newell, *Sidon and Ake*, pl. 1, 4-9 and pl. 5, 16.

Erasure of the symbol from the reverse die of this stater seems pointless. Presumably it had something to do with the basic control system, which required secondary controls only in the case of the small silver. Initial uncertainty as to exactly how the reverses were to be marked is also suggested by the variant form of the monogram on nos. 52 and 54a, the presence of a dot above the strut of the stool on 53 and 54a, and the transposition of symbol and monogram on 54a-b.

Series X. Control: [monogram]

Drachms

Rev. below, [monogram]; to r., club

75. *Rev.* to l., [monogram] erased. *ANS (Sinan), 4.26↑; ANS (Sinan), 4.08↑
76. *Obv.* of 72. *Rev.* no monogram. *Cambridge (*SNGLeake* 2231), 3.98↑
77. *Rev.* as 76. *Commerce 1971
78a. *Rev.* below, [monogram]; no club. *ANS, 4.17↑
b. *Rev.* obscure. ANS, 3.67↑
79a. *ANS, 4.21↑; Oxford (*SNG* 2826), 4.17↑
b. *Rev.* no monogram. ANS, 4.28↑
80. *Obv.* of 68.
a. *ANS (Sinan), 4.19↑; Yale (Bab)
b. ANS (Sinan), 4.08↑

Rev. below, rose

81. *Rev.* to l., [monogram]; below, rose. *ANS, 3.94↑
82. *Rev.* as 81. *Berlin, 4.12
83a. *Rev.* to l., [monogram] erased; below, rose. *ANS (Sinan), 4.22↑
b. *ANS (Sinan), 4.26↑
c. ANS (Asia Minor '64), 4.28↑
d. Egger May 2, 1912, 742, 4.20
84a. *ANS (Sinan), 4.17↑
b. Paris
c. Hersh Coll. (Asia Minor '64), 4.31↑
85a. *ANS (Sinan), 4.28↑
b. ANS (Sinan), 3.98↑
86. ANS, 3.80↑
87. ANS (Larissa), 4.19↑
88. *ANS (Sinan), 4.20↑
89a. ANS (Armenak), 4.23↑
b. Berry Coll., 4.24
90a. *ANS (Sinan), 4.28↑
b. ANS (Sinan), 4.28↑
c. ANS (Sinan), 4.28↑
d. Commerce 1925 (Sinan), 4.25

91a. *ANS (Sinan), 4.27↑
b. ANS (Sinan), 4.28↑
92. *ANS (Larissa), 4.20↑
93. *ANS (Sinan), 4.26↑
94. ANS (*SNGBerry* 258), 4.25↑; Hersh Coll. (Asia Minor '64), 4.30↑

Triobol

Rev. below, rose

95. *Stockholm, 1.88↑

Staters

Rev. to l., Mithras head; to l. below wing, [monogram]

96a. *Rev.* to l. below wing, Mithras head; no monogram. *London.
b. *Saroglos Coll.
97. *Rev.* of 96b. *Berlin, 8.62↑; Hess Dec. 14, 1931, 280, 8.51

Drachms

Rev. to l., Mithras head

98. *Hersh Coll. (Asia Minor '64), 4.30↑
99. *Berlin
100. *ANS (Sinan), 4.27↑
101. *ANS (Sinan), 4.35↑; ANS (Sinan), 4.31↑

Rev. to l., Mithras head; below, [monogram]

102. *Rev.* below, [monogram]. *ANS, 4.13↑
103. *Athens
104. *ANS (Sinan), 4.15↑

Rev. to l., bee; below, [monogram]

105. *Obv.* of 104.
a. *ANS (Sinan), 4.25↑
b. *Rev.* below, [monogram]. Yale (Bab)
106. Petsalis Coll.
107. *Rev.* below, [monogram]. *ANS (Sinan), 4.23↑
108. *Rev.* of 107. ANS, 4.15↑
109. *Rev.* of 107. *ANS (Sinan), 4.25↑
110a. *ANS (Armenak), 4.18↑; Commerce (Asia Minor '61), 4.24↑
b. U.S. Mint
111a. *ANS (Sinan), 4.26↑
b. ANS, 4.13↑
112. *ANS (Sinan), 4.26↑
113a. *ANS (Cavalla), 4.24↑
b. ANS, 4.24↑; ANS, 4.21

Rev. to l., torch; below, |⊙|

114a. *Rev.* below, |⊙|ᑭ. ANS (Larissa), 4.27↑
b. *Rev.* as 114a. London
115. *Rev.* as 114a. *ANS (Sinan), 4.30↑
116a. *Rev.* as 114a. *ANS (Sinan), 4.16↑
b. ANS (Sinan), 4.30↑
117a. *ANS (Sinan), 4.31↑
b. ANS (*SNGBerry* 259), 4.29↑
118a. *ANS (Sinan), 4.22↑
b. ANS (Sinan), 4.26↑
119a. *ANS (Sinan), 4.23↑
b. *Rev.* below, |⊙|ᑭ. Munich
120. *ANS (Sinan), 4.26↑

If there was some evidence of confusion in minting procedure during Series IX, it is even more apparent in the earlier stages of Series X. Assuming that the sequence presented in the catalogue is basically correct, the mint begins by following the pattern of the preceding issue: monogram in the left field with a rose below the stool or a club in the right field. Very soon, however, the monogram is erased from both rose and club dies. The rose is now the sole control on 23 subsequent reverses and the club stands alone on two. When the monogram reappears on the coinage, it is placed below the stool and at least one reverse carries no secondary control (no. 78a) while others have the club in the right field (80a-b) This is the last use of the club as a control on the Sardes coinage; the rose recurs in later issues but it is no longer a dominant symbol.

Meanwhile a third symbol, the Mithras head, is introduced: at first alone on both gold and small silver and then in combination with the monogram.[18] Only seven reverse dies are recorded for drachms before this secondary control, like the club, disappears from the coinage. For the remainder of Series X, a bee or a torch is employed for control purposes.

Two obverse dies of Series IX continue to be used in Series X (72 and 76; 68 and 80). Another obverse (104-5) is shared within Series X by two controls, presumably transferred from Mithras head to bee when the former symbol was abandoned.

[18] Stylistic considerations dictate the separation of the two emissions with a Mithras head as sole control. The obverses of nos. 47-48 of Series VIII are clearly related to the drachm obverses of the two preceding issues, and in one instance die-linked, while nos. 98-101 have obverses similar in style to those of nos. 102-104 with Mithras head left and monogram below the stool.

On the gold of Series VIII, the Mithras head, like earlier symbols, is centered in the left field; in Series X it appears first below Nike's wing (96a) and then is moved to center left to make way for the monogram below the wing (96b). It would seem that the Mithras head was added to the controls of Series X at the time when the mint had temporarily abandoned the monogram and was using a symbol alone. Shortly thereafter, the monogram was reinstated but shifted to the area below the stool for both club and Mithras head drachms, as well as later strikings with bee or torch symbol.

In general the earlier obverses of Series X are stylistically similar to those of Series IX; later stages of emission, marked by bee and torch, produce heads of grosser, less pleasing appearance. On the reverses the figure of Zeus is frequently rendered in an awkward pose with legs far apart, while a few dies show him with crossed legs.[19] Occasionally a true throne with back replaces the customary stool.

Series XI. Control: NK

Staters

Rev. to l., NK ; to r. below wing, torch

121. *ANS, 8.52↑; Kelly June 1, 1953, 958

Drachms

Rev. to l., NK; below, torch

122. *Rev.* NK cut over [monogram]; below monogram, torch. *ANS (Sinan), 4.27↑
123. ANS (Cavalla), 4.08↑
124. Yale (Bab)
125. *Hersh Coll. (Asia Minor '64), 4.30↑
126. *Rev.* NK . *ANS (Sinan), 4.26↑
127. *Rev.* as 126. ANS (Armenak), 4.14↑
128. *Rev.* as 126. *Petsalis Coll.; Oxford (*SNG* 2829),4.17↑
129. *Rev.* as 126. *Mass. Hist. Soc.
130. *ANS (Sinan), 4.32↑

131a. *Rev.* to l., torch (?) below NK. ANS, 4.17↑
  b. *Rev.* as 131a. Hermitage
  c. *Rev.* to l., torch below NK. *ANS (Armenak), 4.20↑; ANS, 4.25↑

Rev. to l., NK and rose

132a. *Rev.* to l., NK in exergue, rose. *Vienna, 4.02
  b. *Rev.* monogram may be recut. *ANS (Cavalla), 4.13↑; ANS, 3.97↑
  c. ANS, 4.18↑; Berry Coll., 4.16; Berlin

133a. *Rev.* of 132c. *ANS (Sinan), 4.26↑
  b. Hermitage
  c. Vinchon Apr. 6, 1959, 30, 4.10

19 On two earlier reverses (nos. 47-48) the legs are also crossed as they are on nos. 119a and 120, but other reverses from the same obverse dies have the usual representation of parallel legs (nos. 43 and 119b).

This peculiar rendering of a spread-lap Zeus is found on coins of Lampsacus and Abydus but not elsewhere among the Asia Minor mints.

Rev. to l., NK and bee

134. *ANS (Sinan), 4.26↑
135. *ANS (Sinan), 4.18↓
136a. *Rev.* ИK. *ANS (Sinan), 4.25↑
 b. ANS (Cavalla), 4.15↑
137. *Rev.* ИK. *ANS (Sinan), 4.27↑; Athens
138. *ANS (Sinan), 4.29↑
139. *ANS (*SNGBerry* 260), 4.25↑
140. Athens (Corinth), 4.24
141. *Hermitage
142. *ANS (Sinan), 4.22↓
143a. *Rev.* of 142. *ANS (Sinan), 4.28↓
 b. Oxford (*SNG* 2827), 4.12↑
144a. *ANS (Armenak), 4.04↑
 b. ANS, 4.07↑
145a. *ANS (Sinan), 4.28↑
 b. ANS, 4.28↑
 c. Auctiones A.G. Sept. 30, 1976, 109, 4.29

With Series XI the control monogram returns to the left field. Secondary controls of rose, bee and torch carry over from the preceding issue, and these are now often placed directly below the monogram. The recutting on the reverse of no. 122 more likely indicates initial uncertainty as to what the basic annual control would be rather than the reuse of an old die.[20]

There is no transfer of dies from Series X but the stylistic characteristics of its bee and torch dies are repeated on the obverses and reverses of Series XI.

Series XII. Control: ጥ

Staters

Rev. ΦΙΛΙΠΠΟΥ; to l., ጥ and torch

146. *Obv.* of 121
 a. *Rev.* ΑΛΕΞΑΝΔΡΟΥ. *ANS (= Glendining May 27, 1936, 49), 8.53↑
 b. Cambridge (*SNGLeake* 2253), 8.56↑
 c. *London
147. *Rev.* of 146c. *Paris
148. *Commerce (Paeonia), 8.56↑

[20] The slouched, spread-lap Zeus of no. 122 has no parallel on the drachms of the earlier 㐬 issue. The same monogram, however, is used for a later series and may have been originally intended as the control for the present emission.

Drachms

Rev. to l., ᛗ and torch

149. *Obv.* of 131
 a. *London
 b. Commerce (Asia Minor '61)
150. *Obv.* of 145. *Rev.* ΦΙΛΙΠΠΟΥ; below, monogram. *ANS (Sinan), 4.25↑
151. *Rev.* ᛗ cut over NK (?); below, torch. *Vienna
152a. *ANS (Sinan), 4.28↑
 b. *Rev.* ΦΙΛΙΠΠΟΥ. London
 c. *Rev.* as 152b. Paris
153a. *Rev.* of 152c. ANS (Sinan), 4.30↑
 b. *ANS (Sinan), 4.25↑
154a. *ANS (Armenak), 4.30↑
 b. ANS, 4.25↑
155. *Stockholm, 4.12↑
156a. *ANS (Sinan), 4.32↑
 b. ANS, 4.27↑
157. *Rev.* ΦΙΛΙΠΠΟΥ; below, monogram. *ANS, 4.29↑
158a. *Rev.* as 157 but monogram blundered. ANS, 4.22↑
 b. *Rev.* as 157. *London
159a. *Rev.* ΦΙΛΙΠΠΟΥ. *ANS (Sinan), 4.28↑
 b. ANS (Armenak), 4.15↑
160. *Rev.* ΦΙΛΙΠΠΟΥ; below, monogram. *ANS (Armenak), 4.17↑
161. *Rev.* of 160. ANS (Armenak), 4.18↑
162. *Rev.* as 160. *ANS (Larissa), 4.17↑

Rev. ΦΙΛΙΠΠΟΥ; to l., rose; below, ᛗ

163a. *ANS, 4.26↑; ANS, 4.21↑
 b. Naville 1, Apr. 4, 1921, 953, 4.22
164. *ANS, 4.22↑
165. *London; Oxford (*SNG* 3196), 4.08↑
166. *Rev.* ΑΛΕΞΑΝΔΡΟΥ; to l., monogram and rose. *ANS, 4.03↑
167. *Rev.* as 166. *Berlin, 4.10↑
168. *Rev.* ΑΛΕΞΑΝΔΡΟΥ; to l., ›E; below, rose. *Gotha

For the first time at Sardes, coinage is struck with the names of both Philip III and Alexander IV in roughly equal proportions. There seems to have been no attempt at segregation, either by symbol or by obverse die. Torch and rose serve as secondary controls for drachms with both inscriptions and the same obverse die is shared by Alexander and Philip reverses. Only with respect to the placement of monogram and symbol is there any evidence of differentiation: on drachms with Alexander reverses the two controls are generally combined in the left field, on Philip reverses the symbol is usually in the left field and the monogram below the stool.

One stater and two drachm dies are carried over from Series XI. In the case of no. 150, there is a distinct die break at the outer corner of the eye, which is not visible on no. 145. What is almost certainly a cutting of [monogram] over [monogram] on no. 151 provides further support for the sequence of issues.

Series XIII. Control: [monogram]

Staters

Rev. to l., [monogram] and torch

169. *Obv.* of 148(?).[21] *Rev.* ΦΙΛΙΠΠΟΥ. *ANS, 8.52↑; London
170. *Agora Excavations; Istanbul, 8.53↑

Rev. to l., [monogram] and acrostolion

171. *Munich; Kress 154, Mar. 21, 1972, 134, 8.50
172a. *Berlin; Hermitage, 8.52↑; Commerce 1923, 8.48
b. ANS, 8.53↑
c. *Obv.* die recut. *London; Santamaria Oct. 12, 1949, 29, 8.58
173. *Rev.* to l., [monogram]; r., acrostolion. *London; Gotha

Distater

Rev. to l., [monogram] and acrostolion

174. *Godefroid Coll. 1934

Drachms[22]

Rev. to l., [monogram]; below, rose

175. *Berry Coll., 4.15

Rev. to l., [monogram] and bee

176. *ANS (Armenak), 4.25↑
177. ANS, 4.13↑
178. *Rev.* ΦΙΛΙΠΠΟΥ; to l., monogram; below, bee. *The Hague
179a. *Rev.* of 178. ANS, 4.22↑
b. *Rev.* ΦΙΛΙΠΠΟΥ; to l., bee; below, [monogram]. *ANS (Sinan), 4.28↑; ANS (Cavalla), 4.10↑; ANS (Larissa), 4.19↑
180. *Rev.* as 179b but with [monogram]. *ANS (Sinan), 4.30↑; London

[21] The photograph in the Parke Bernet catalogue is so poor that it is impossible to be sure of the die identity.

[22] In cases where the monogram is partly off flan, it has been assumed that the usual [monogram] form was used.

Rev. to l., 䍘 and upright torch

181.[23] *Rev.* to l., 羊; to r., torch. *ANS, 3.90↑
182a. *ANS (Sinan), 4.25↑
b. ANS (Sinan), 4.25↑
c. ANS, 4.21↑
183a. *Rev.* 羊. *Myers Dec. 5, 1974, 72 (Asia Minor '61), 4.31
b. *Rev.* as 183a. Hersh Coll. (Asia Minor '64), 4.34↑
184a. *ANS (Sinan), 4.18↑
b. ANS (Sinan), 4.18↑
c. *Rev.* 羊. ANS, 4.05↑
185. ANS, 3.69↑
186a. *ANS (Sinan), 4.34↑
b. ANS (Sinan), 4.30↑
c. Paris, 4.30↑
d. Schlessinger Feb. 4, 1935, 713, 4.10
187. *Rev.* of 186d. *ANS (Sinan), 4.30↑
188a. *ANS (*SNGBerry* 261), 4.25↑
b. ANS (Sinan), 4.26↑
189. *Rev.* symbol above monogram. *ANS (Sinan), 4.26↑
190a. *ANS (Sinan), 4.30↑
b. ANS (Sinan), 4.16↑

Rev. to l., 䍘; below, horizontal torch

191. *Obv.* of 190. *ANS, 4.22↑
192a. *ANS (Sinan), 4.26↑; ANS (Sinan), 4.28↑
b. Hersh Coll. (Asia Minor '64), 4.27↑
c. ANS (Armenak), 4.14↑
193. *Rev.* of 192c. ANS, 4.22↑
194a. *Rev.* of 192b. *ANS (Cavalla), 4.15↑
b. ANS, 4.08↑
c. Copenhagen (*SNG* 904), 3.96↑
195. *Rev.* symbol omitted. *ANS (Sinan), 4.17↑
196a. *ANS (Sinan), 4.28↑
b. ANS (Sinan), 4.28↑
c. ANS (Sinan), 4.29↑
d. ANS (Olympia), 4.16↑
e. ANS (Larissa), 4.21↑
197. *ANS (Armenak), 4.23↑
198. ANS (Sinan), 4.31↑
199a. *ANS (Sinan), 4.28↑; ANS (Armenak), 4.19↑; London
b. ANS (Sinan), 4.14↑

[23] Possibly the same obverse die as no. 182; the condition of the single specimen makes certainty impossible.

Rev. ΦΙΛΙΠΠΟΥ; to l., [monogram]; below, horse's leg

200. *Rev.* symbol in exergue. *Cambridge (*SNGLeake* 2278), 4.21↑
201a. *Rev.* of 200. Oxford (*SNG* 3197), 4.01↑
b. *ANS, 4.09↑
202. *ANS, 4.21↑
203. *ANS (Sinan), 4.26↑; ANS (Larissa), 4.14↑; London

Rev. ΦΙΛΙΠΠΟΥ; to l., [monogram]; below, upright torch

204. *Zara Coll., 4.09↑
205. *ANS, 4.25↑
206. *Rev.* [monogram]. ANS, 4.03↑
207. *Rev.* as 206. *ANS (Armenak), 4.19↑

Rev. ΦΙΛΙΠΠΟΥ; to l., upright torch, below, [monogram]

208. *Obv.* of 202. *ANS (Sinan), 4.29↑; ANS (Sinan), 4.26↑; Helbing Mar. 20, 1928, 197, 4.25
209. *ANS, 4.21↑
210. *Rev.* [monogram]. *ANS (Sinan), 4.27↑

Rev. ΦΙΛΙΠΠΟΥ; to l., ΤΙ above [monogram]; below, upright torch

211. *Obv.* of 209.
a. *ANS (Larissa), 4.15↑
b. The Hague
212. *ANS (Sinan), 4.30↑
213. *ANS (Sinan), 4.29↑; ANS, 4.12↑
214. *Obv.* of 202.
a. *ANS (Larissa), 4.12↑; ANS (Larissa), 4.18↑; ANS (Armenak), 4.04↑
b. ANS (Armenak), 4.21↑
c. ANS (Sinan), 4.25↑
d. ANS (Mesopot. '20), 4.07↑

Bronze Units

Obv. Shield with caduceus in center

Rev. ΒΑ and helmet; to l., caduceus; to r., rose

215. *Rev.* symbols transposed. *ANS, 3.61↑
216. *Rev.* [monogram] below caduceus. *ANS, 4.38↑
217. *Rev.* ΤΙ and [monogram] below caduceus. *ANS, 4.13↑

Series XIII has the same basic control as Series IX but even a cursory glance at the plates reveals the marked stylistic difference between the two emissions. After several years of rather modest operation, production is increased: at least 36 obverse dies are used for drachms and five for staters, of which two (nos. 170-71) are very close in style to the earlier no. 146 and a third (no. 169) may be a transfer from Series XII. A surprising addition to the output of gold is the distater denomination, known for Miletus but otherwise unattested at our Asia Minor mints.[24] Bronzes are also struck but the types are now shield/helmet instead of the Heracles head/bow and club of prior issues.

Two new symbols are employed along with the familiar rose, bee and torch: the acrostolion for gold and the horse's leg for small silver. As in Series XII, there is a fairly even division of coinage between Philip III and Alexander IV but almost all gold carries the inscription ΑΛΕΞΑΝΔΡΟΥ. On the evidence of the present record, which may be misleading since it is obviously incomplete, the acrostolion and rose seem to have been reserved for coins with the name of Alexander, while the horse's leg is used only with Philip reverses.

The bee is shared but, following the general pattern of Series XII, the symbol and monogram are combined in the left field for Alexander and separated for Philip. Similarly there are variations in the location and representation of the torch, the major symbol of the issue, which appear to be related to the inscription. Alexander's coins either have an upright torch and the monogram together in the left field or the monogram alone to left and a horizontal torch below the stool. On Philip's money the symbol and monogram are also separated but the torch is invariably upright.

Reverses of the two rulers do not share a common obverse die; when linkage occurs it involves reverses of somewhat different format but with the same name. For example, nos. 202, 208, 214, as well as 261 of Series XIV, are from a single obverse die. Although the reverse markings are diverse, all coins are inscribed ΦΙΛΙΠΠΟΥ.

Eight reverses of the Philip sequence have ΤΙ in addition to ≢ as the basic control and a bronze piece (no. 217) is marked in the same fashion. Unmistakably these coins link Series XIII and XIV but whether they belong at the end of one issue or the beginning of the next is quite uncertain.

Series XIV. Control: ΤΙ

Staters

Rev. to l., ΤΙ and torch

218. *Rev.* ΦΙΛΙΠΠΟΥ; to l., ΤΙ with ≢ below wing erased; to r., torch. *ANS, 8.48↑; Bourgey June 13, 1977, 33, 8.58

219a. *London

b. *Rev.* ΤΙ in circle. Hermitage

220a. *Rev.* of 219a. *ANS, 8.56↑

b. *Rev.* as 219b. Berlin

221. *Obv.* on helmet, griffin

a. *Rev.* as 219b. *ANS, 8.49↑; London (Larnaca); Athens

b. *Rev.* as 219b. ANS, 8.53↑; Glasgow, 8.42

[24] No. 174 reproduces a cast from Newell's trays, labelled "Gotefroid Collection 1934". The present whereabouts of the coin are unknown. A second specimen from the same pair of dies has recently appeared (Leu 28, May 5, 1981, 85).

c. *Rev.* ΒΑΣΙΛΕΩΣ ΑΛΕΞΑΝΔΡΟΥ; to l., torch; to r., ΤΙ. Paris
d. *Rev.* as 221c. Saroglos Coll.; London
e. *Rev.* as 221c. Berlin (Larnaca); London (Larnaca); Hermitage (Anadol), 8.52↑ Oxford (*SNG* 2824), 8.54↑; J. Schulman Feb. 4, 1957, 1206 (= Ciani-Vinchon May 6, 1955, 205)
f. *Rev.* as 221c. *ANS (= Ratto May 16, 1935, 5), 8.56↑

Rev. to l., ΤΙ and bird

222. *London
223. *Rev.* of 222. *Saroglos Coll.

Rev. to l., ΤΙ in circle[25] and ivy leaf

224a. *ANS, 8.53↑
b. ANS, 8.42↑
c. London; Berlin (Larnaca)
d. *Rev.* to l., ΤΙ in circle; to r., ivy leaf. Saroglos Coll.; Oxford (*SNG* 2823), 8.55↑; G. Hirsch Dec. 11, 1967, 2090, 8.47

Rev. to l., ΤΙ and bee

225. *Obv.* of 224
a. London (Larnaca)
b. London
c. *ANS, 8.38↑
d. *Rev.* ΦΙΛΙΠΠΟΥ. Athens (Thoricos), 8.58

Rev. ΦΙΛΙΠΠΟΥ; to l., ΤΙ and star

226. *ANS, 8.56↑
227. *Rev.* to l., ΤΙ; to r., star. *London

Rev. ΦΙΛΙΠΠΟΥ; to l., ΤΙ and rose

228. *Commerce 1951
229. *Turin, 8.52
230. *Rev.* of 229. *Commerce (Paeonia), 8.55↑

Tetradrachms

Rev. to l., rose; below, ΤΙ

231. *Phillips Coll. (Abu Hommos)

Rev. to l., ΤΙ; below, ivy leaf

232. *Obv.* of 231
a. ANS, 17.10↑
b. *Phillips Coll. (Abu Hommos)
c. Commerce 1971, 16.96

[25] The circle is sometimes dotted.

233. *ANS, 17.01↑
234a. *Rev.* of 233. *ANS, 16.88↑; London
b. Oxford (Kuft; *SNG* 2834), 17.17↑
c. Commerce 1968
235a. *Oxford (Kuft; *SNG* 2833), 17.08↑
b. Hollschek Coll., 17.01

Rev. to l., torch; below, TI

236a. *ANS, 16.96↑
b. Commerce (Asia Minor '70), 16.88↑
237a. *ANS (Kuft), 17.19↑; Vienna
b. ANS, 17.03↑
238a. *Berlin
b. Oxford (Kuft; *SNG* 2837), 17.05↑
c. Yale Univ., 17.05↑
239a. ANS, 16.28↑
b. Oxford (Kuft,; *SNG* 2838), 17.07↑
c. ANS, 16.91↑
d. ANS, 16.77↑
e. Peus FPL 29, July 1972, 8
f. Alexandria
g. *Vienna; London (Kuft)
240. *Rev.* filleted torch. *ANS, 17.13↓
241. *Rev.* ΦΙΛΙΠΠΟΥ. *London
242. *Rev.* as 241. *London

Drachms

Rev. ΦΙΛΙΠΠΟΥ; to l., TI

243.[26] *ANS, 4.23↑; *Commerce (Asia Minor '61), 4.24↑

Rev. ΦΙΛΙΠΠΟΥ; to l., TI; below, horse's leg

244. *Obv.* of 203. *ANS, 4.10↑

Rev. ΦΙΛΙΠΠΟΥ; to l., TI above star

245. *London
246a. *ANS (Sinan), 4.25↑
b. ANS (Sinan), 4.27↑
c. *Rev.* to l., star above TI. *ANS (Sinan), 4.27↑

[26] This is a peculiar striking. The hoard coin, with a die-break below the lion's jaw, has no trace of any marking below the throne. On the ANS piece, which should be the earlier since its obverse shows no die-break, there seems to be an erasure below the throne. Curious flaws on its reverse surface suggest the use of an old flan with inadequate erasure. The style of the obverse is closest to no. 249.

Rev. ΦΙΛΙΠΠΟΥ; to l., rose; below, ΤΙ

247. *ANS (Sinan), 4.28↑; ANS, 4.20↑
248a. ANS, 3.68↑; Copenhagen (*SNG* 1095), 4.15↑
b. *Rev.* to l., ΤΙ; below, rose. *ANS, 4.31↑
249. *Rev.* as 248b. *ANS (Sinan), 4.27↑

Rev. to l., ΤΙ above bird

250. *Rev.* ΦΙΛΙΠΠΟΥ; to l., bird; below, ΤΙ. *ANS (*SNGBerry* 264), 4.27↑
251. *Rev.* as 250. *ANS, 4.19↑
252. *Rev.* ΦΙΛΙΠΠΟΥ. *ANS (Cavalla), 4.19↑; ANS, 4.02↑
253a. *Rev.* as 252. Oxford (*SNG* 3199), 4.17↑
b. *Rev.* as 252. *ANS, 3.89↑
254a. *Rev.* of 253b. *ANS (Cavalla), 4.17↑
b. *ANS (Armenak), 4.13↑
255a. *Rev.* of 254b. *ANS (Sinan), 4.27↑
b. *Rev.* ΦΙΛΙΠΠΟΥ inscribed upward. *ANS (Sinan), 4.31↑
256. *ANS (Sinan), 4.27↑
257a. *Rev.* ΦΙΛΙΠΠΟΥ. Copenhagen (*SNG* 1098), 4.19↑
b. *ANS (Cavalla), 4.25↑
258a. *Rev.* of 257b. ANS (Sinan), 4.28↑
b. ANS (Sinan), 4.25↑; ANS (Larissa), 4.17↑
c. *ANS, 4.29↑
d. ANS (Sinan), 4.25↑
259a. *Rev.* of 258d. *Istanbul (Izmit), 4.27↑
b. ANS (Sinan), 4.27↑; ANS, 4.07↑
260. *Berne

Rev. ΦΙΛΙΠΠΟΥ; to l., torch; below, ΤΙ

261. *Obv.* of 202. *Rev.* to l., ΤΙ; below, torch. *ANS (Sinan), 4.29↑
262. *Obv.* of 213. *Rev.* as 261. *ANS (Sinan), 4.29↑; ANS, 3.91↑; London
263. *Rev.* of 262. *ANS (Larissa), 4.15↑
264. *Obv.* of 255
a. *Rev.* to l., ΤΙ above torch. *ANS (Sinan), 4.23↑
b. *Rev.* as 264a. ANS (Sinan), 4.28↑
265. *Obv.* of 253. *Rev.* of 264b. *ANS (Sinan), 4.30↑
266. *Obv.* of 254. *Rev.* as 264a. *ANS (Cavalla), 4.16↑
267. *Rev.* as 264a. *ANS (Armenak), 4.12↑
268. *Rev.* as 264a. *London
269. *Obv.* of 210. *London
270. *Obv.* of 207. *ANS, 4.29↑
271. *ANS (Mosul '17), 4.07↑; The Hague
272a. *Rev.* to l., ΤΙ; below, torch. *ANS (Cavalla), 4.11↑
b. ANS (Cavalla), 4.16↑

273a. *ANS (Sinan), 4.28↑
b. ANS, 4.24↑
274. *Rev.* of 273b. *Schlessinger Feb. 4, 1935, 752, 4.10
275. *Rev.* of 273b. *Cambridge (*SNGLeake* 2277), 4.15↑
275A. ANS (Cavalla), 4.16↑
276a. ANS, 3.92↑; Superior Stamp and Coin June 17, 1974, 163
b. ANS (Armenak), 4.17↑; Naville 1, Apr. 4, 1921, 952, 4.09
c. *ANS (Sinan), 4.30↑; Copenhagen (*SNG* 1092), 4.18↑
277a. *Rev.* of 276c. ANS (Sinan), 4.28↑
b. *Rev.* of 276b. *ANS (Sinan), 4.28↑

Rev. to l., TI; below, bee

278a. *ANS (Sinan), 4.26↑; ANS (Sinan), 4.30↑; ANS (Sinan), 4.28↑
b. ANS (Cavalla), 4.17↑; ANS (Cavalla), 4.19↑; Commerce (Asia Minor '61)
c. ANS (Sinan), 4.30↑
d. ANS (Sinan), 4.26↑
e. ANS (Sinan), 4.20↑
f. ANS, 4.02↑
g. Commerce (Sinan), 4.29
h. ANS (Sinan), 4.31↑
i. Athens
279a. *Rev.* of 278i. *ANS (Sinan), 4.32↑
b. *Rev.* of 278h. ANS (Armenak), 4.20↑
c. ANS (Sinan), 4.34↑
d. *Rev.* to l., TI above bee. *ANS (Sinan), 4.30↑; ANS (Sinan), 4.28↑; ANS (Sinan), 4.29↑; London
e. *Rev.* as 279d. ANS, 4.29↑
280a. *Rev.* of 278f. *ANS (Sinan), 4.24↑; ANS (Sinan), 4.32↑; ANS, 4.12↑
b. ANS (Sinan), 4.25↑
c. *Rev.*: to l., TI above bee. ANS (Armenak), 4.14↑; Münz. u. Med. FPL 317, Oct. 1970, 9, 4.31; Cahn 75, May 30, 1932, 289 (= J. Schulman, June 8, 1931, 94), 4.30
d. *Rev.* to l., bee above TI. *ANS (Sinan), 4.30↑
e. *Rev.* as 280d. ANS (*SNGBerry* 263), 4.22↑
281. *ANS (*SNGBerry* 262), 4.27↑
282. *ANS (Cavalla), 4.22↑; ANS, 4.25↑
283a. ANS (Sinan), 4.29↑
b. *Rev.* to l., bee above TI. *ANS (Sinan), 4.30↑
284a. *Rev.* to l., bee; below, TI. ANS (Sinan), 4.28↑
b. *Rev.* to l., bee above TI. *ANS (Sinan), 4.29↑; ANS (Sinan), 4.29↑
c. *Rev.* as 284b. Vienna
285a. *Rev.* of 284c. ANS, 4.01↑
b. *Rev.* of 284b. ANS (Cavalla), 4.20↑
c. *Rev.* as 285b. *ANS (Sinan), 4.28↑

286a. *Rev.* to l., bee above TI. *ANS (Sinan), 4.30↑; ANS (Sinan), 4.32↑
b. *Rev.* as 286a. ANS (Armenak), 4.24↑; ANS (Sinan), 4.27↑
287a. *Rev.* to l., bee above TI. *ANS (Sinan), 4.27↑; ANS (Sinan), 4.31↑
b. *Rev.* as 287a. ANS (Sinan), 4.29↑; Cahn 84, Nov. 29, 1933, 255[27] (= Naville 15, July 2, 1930, 501), 4.24
c. *Rev.* as 287a. ANS, 4.28↑; Rome (Terme)
288a. *Rev.* of 287c. *ANS (Sinan), 4.26↑
b. *Rev.* of 287b. ANS, 4.09↑
c. *Rev.* of 287a. ANS (Sinan), 4.27↑; Auctiones AG Sept. 30, 1976, 110, 4.26
d. ANS (Sinan), 4.28↑
289a. ANS, 4.21↑
b. *Rev.* ΦΙΛΙΠΠΟΥ. *ANS (Sinan), 4.30↑
290a. *Rev.* ΦΙΛΙΠΠΟΥ; to l., bee; below, TI. *ANS (Sinan), 4.22↑; Hermitage
b. *Rev.* as 290a. ANS (Sinan), 3.86↑
c. *Rev.* as 290a. ANS (Sinan), 4.26↑
291. *Rev.* as 290a. *ANS (Larissa), 4.19↑
292a. *Rev.* ΦΙΛΙΠΠΟΥ; to l., TI above bee. *ANS (Sinan), 4.27↑
b. *Rev.* to l., bee above TI. ANS (Sinan), 4.27↑; Berry Coll.
c. *Rev.* as 292b. ANS (Sinan), 4.28↑
d. *Rev.* as 292b. ANS, 4.01↓
e. *Rev.* to l., TI above bee. ANS, 3.98↑
f. London
293a. *Rev.* ΦΙΛΙΠΠΟΥ; to l., TI above bee. ANS (Cavalla), 4.18↑; U.S.Mint
b. *Rev.* to l., TI above bee. ANS, 4.30↑
c. *Rev.* to l., bee above TI. *ANS (Sinan), 4.31↑
d. *Rev.* as 293c. ANS (Armenak), 4.21↑
e. *Rev.* as 293c. ANS, 4.31↑; ANS, 4.14↑
f. *Rev.* to l., TI; below, bee. ANS (Sinan), 4.30↑
g. *Rev.* as 293f. ANS (Sinan), 4.28↑
294a. *Rev.* of 293g. ANS (Cavalla), 4.22↑
b. *Rev.* as 294a. Hesperia Art Bulletin 4, 4
c. *Rev.* to l., bee above TI. *ANS (Sinan), 4.28↑; Copenhagen (*SNG* 961), 4.08↑; Oxford (*SNG* 2836), 4.26↑
d. *Rev.* as 294c. ANS (Armenak), 4.21↓; ANS (Sinan), 4.28↓
e. *Rev.* as 294c. ANS, 4.17↑

Bronze Units

Obv. Shield with caduceus in center

Rev. BA and helmet; below, caduceus, TI and rose

295. *ANS, 3.75←
296. *ANS, 4.27↖

[27] Misnumbered on the plate as 256.

After several emissions with little gold and no tetradrachms, the mint drastically increases production with Series XIV. Twelve obverse dies for staters are on record and eleven for tetradrachms, heretofore a very rare denomination at Sardes. Drachms are plentiful and there is some bronze of the shield/helmet variety. New subsidiary controls appear: bird, ivy-leaf and star supplement the rose, bee, torch and horse's leg of earlier strikings. Coinage continues to be issued for both Philip and Alexander and there is some evidence of systematic differentiation on the basis of symbols. Philip's gold is generally marked with rose or star; most of his small silver is associated with rose, star, horse's leg or torch. Alexander's name is found on practically all tetradrachms and on the majority of the drachms which carry the bird or bee symbol. An obverse die is occasionally shared by Philip and Alexander reverses.[28]

No. 221 is unusual in two respects. A griffin replaces the customary serpent on Athena's helmet and four of the six recorded reverses are inscribed ΒΑΣΙΛΕΩΣ ΑΛΕΞΑΝΔΡΟΥ, the first appearance of the royal title at Sardes. Certain stylistic developments are also noteworthy. For the most part Nike is still rendered in a rigid standing position, but on a few reverses she is definitely advancing left. On all tetradrachms and the majority of the drachms Zeus is now shown in relaxed pose with legs crossed; the grotesque spread-lap representation of earlier issues has disappeared.

Series XIV is linked to Series XIII by five transferred drachm dies (nos. 244, 261-62, 269-70). Within the ΤΙ emission itself, reverses with different symbols sometimes share an obverse die: ivy-leaf and bee for staters; rose and ivy-leaf for tetradrachms; bird and torch for drachms.

Series XV. Control: Α

Staters

Rev. to l., torch; to r., Α

297. *Obv.* of 230. *Rev.* ΦΙΛΙΠΠΟΥ; to l., Α above torch. *ANS (= Sotheby July 6, 1921, 228), 8.52↑; Coin Galleries FPL 2, 1962, B4, 8.58
298. *Rev.* of 297. *London; Hermitage (Anadol); Commerce (Paeonia), 8.51↑
299. *Paris
300a. *Rev.* down to l., ΒΑΣΙΛΕΩΣ (retrograde). *Cambridge (*SNGLeake* 2095), 8.47←
b. *Rev.* down to l., probably ΒΑΣΙΛΕΩΣ. Vienna, 8.41
301a. *ANS, 8.54↑
b. London; Berry Coll., 8.53↑; G. Hirsch Sept. 20, 1956, 28
302. *Rev.* of 301b. *Berlin
303a. *ANS, 8.56↑
b. *London
c. *Rev.* down to l., ΒΑΣΙΛΕΩΣ. Hermitage, 8.49↑
d. *Rev.* down to r., ΒΑΣΙΛΕΩΣ; down to l., ΑΕΞΑΝ [*sic*]. Glendining May 14, 1957, 701, 8.43

[28] For example, nos. 225, 255, 289, 292-93.

Philip II Stater

Rev. below horses, Α and torch

304. *Munich

Tetradrachms

Rev. ΦΙΛΙΠΠΟΥ; to l., rose; below, Α

305a. *ANS, 17.10↑; ANS, 16.72↑; London; Myers-Adams Dec. 6, 1973, 97, 17.00
b. *Rev.* Α. Alexandria; Sternberg Nov. 24, 1977, 83, 17.14
c. *ANS, 17.14↑; Hamburger Apr. 3, 1933, 520, 17.12
306. *Riechmann 30, Dec. 11, 1924, 471, 17.15

Rev. ΦΙΛΙΠΠΟΥ; to l., torch; below, Α

307. *Obv.* of 242. *Private Coll., Cairo (Abu Hommos)
308a. *London
b. *Rev.* to l., filleted torch. *Lyons; Commerce before 1941
309. *Rev.* ΑΛΕΞΑΝΔΡΟΥ; below, ΑΘ. *Alexandria
310. *Rev.* ΑΛΕΞΑΝΔΡΟΥ. *London

Drachms[29]

Rev. ΦΙΛΙΠΠΟΥ; to l., rose; below, Α

311. *ANS (Sinan), 4.28↑; ANS (Sinan), 4.13↑
312a. *Rev.* of 311. *ANS (Sinan), 4.31↑
b. ANS (Armenak), 4.13↑
313a. *ANS (Cavalla), 4.23↑
b. ANS (Sinan), 4.28↑; ANS, 4.24↑
c. Athens; Dewing Coll.

Rev. to l., bee; below, Α

314a. *Rev.* ΦΙΛΙΠΠΟΥ. *ANS (Armenak), 4.19↑; London
b. *Rev.* as 314a. ANS (Armenak), 4.19↑
c. *Rev.* as 314a. Oxford (*SNG* 3200), 4.09↑
315. *Rev.* as 314a. *ANS (Armenak), 4.14↑; ANS, 4.10↑
316. *Rev.* as 314a. ANS, 4.22↑
317. *Obv.* of 294
a. *Rev.* to l., Α cut over bee above ΤΙ; below, bee. *ANS (Armenak), 4.31↑; ANS (Larissa), 4.13↑; ANS (Armenak), 4.23↑; ANS, 4.19↑; Hermitage
b. *Rev.* symbol and monogram transposed. ANS (Armenak), 4.16↑
c. *Rev.* as 317b. ANS, 4.08↑
318. *Obv.* of 293. *Rev.* as 317b. *ANS, 4.24↑

[29] On the drachm reverses the dot of the Α is often omitted or misplaced (Α).

319a. *Rev.* as 317b. *ANS (Armenak), 4.19↑
b. *Rev.* as 317b. ANS (Armenak), 4.17↑; Phar Coll.
320a. *Rev.* as 317b. *London
b. *Rev.* to l., large bee horizontally r. *London
321a. *ANS (Armenak), 4.18↑
b. *Rev.* as 317b. Oxford (*SNG* 2839), 4.22↑

Rev. to l., torch; below, A

322. *Obv.* of 277. *Rev.* ΦΙΛΙΠΠΟΥ. *ANS (Sinan), 4.28↑
323. *Rev.* of 322. *Ratto Feb. 8, 1928, 310, 4.28; Copenhagen (*SNG* 1091), 4.06↑
324a. *Rev.* ΦΙΛΙΠΠΟΥ. *ANS, 4.20↑
b. *Rev.* as 324a. ANS (Sinan), 4.30↑
c. *Rev.* as 324a. ANS, 4.03↑
d. *Rev.* as 324a. Ratto Apr. 4, 1927, 709, 4.27

Obv. die recut.

e. *Rev.* as 324a. ANS, 4.14↑
f. *Rev.* as 324a. ANS, 4.26↑
g. *Rev.* as 324a. Turin
325. *Rev.* as 324a. ANS, 4.07↑
326. *Rev.* as 324a. *ANS (Sinan), 4.27↑
327. *Rev.* as 324a. *London
328. *Obv.* of 321. *ANS (Armenak), 4.19↑
329. *Rev.* to l., torch above A. *ANS (Armenak), 4.05↑
330.[30] *ANS (Cavalla), 3.76 (plated?) →
331. *ANS (Cavalla), 4.19↑
332. *ANS (Larissa), 4.15↑
333a. *ANS (Cavalla), 4.20↑
b. ANS, 3.99↑
c. Athens (Corinth)
334a. *Rev.* to l., torch above A. *ANS (*SNGBerry* 265), 4.29↑; Commerce (Asia Minor '61)
b. ANS, 4.28↑; Cambridge (*SNGLeake* 2194), 4.17↑
c. ANS, 4.17↑
335. *ANS, 3.88↑
336a. *ANS (Cavalla), 4.18↓
b. ANS (Cavalla), 4.20 ←
c. Cambridge (Grose 3484), 4.15 →
d. Cambridge (Grose 3500), 4.18↑
337. *Commerce (Asia Minor '61)
338. *ANS, 4.25↑

[30] This crude and apparently plated coin may be an imitation.

339a. *ANS, 4.28↑
b. The Hague
c. G. Hirsch Apr. 4, 1960, 139
340. *ANS, 3.97↓
341. *Berry Coll., 4.18
342. Oxford (Davidson)
343a. *Rev.* from l. below, ΒΑΣΙΛΕΩΣ. *ANS, 4.17←; Paris
b. ANS, 4.04→
344a. *ANS (Cavalla), 4.13↓
b. ANS (Cavalla), 4.03↓
c. ANS, 4.27↓
d. ANS, 4.14↓
345a. *Rev.* of 344d. *Commerce (Asia Minor '61); ANS, 4.15→
b. ANS, 4.25←
c. *ANS (Armenak), 4.14←; ANS (Cavalla), 4.11←
346a. *Rev.* of 344d. ANS (Mesopot. '20), 4.05↑
b. *ANS (Mosul '17), 3.99↓
c. ANS (Mosul '17), 4.13↓
347a. *ANS (Armenak), 4.14←
b. ANS (Larissa), 4.19→
c. ANS, 4.22←; Glendining June 21, 1972, 148, 4.22
d. ANS (Mesopot. '20), 4.16→
e. ANS, 4.14←
f. ANS, 4.17←
348. *ANS, 4.18↓
349. Cambridge (*SNGLeake* 2195), 4.08↑
350a. *ANS (Larissa), 4.26↑
b. ANS, 4.15↑
351a. *ANS, 4.28↑
b. ANS (Larissa), 4.11↑
352a. *Commerce (Asia Minor '61)
b. Commerce (Asia Minor '61)
353a. *Hermitage
b. ANS (Cavalla), 4.18↑; Kricheldorf Oct. 15, 1955, 256, 4.22
354a. *ANS (Armenak), 4.23↑
b. ANS, 4.21↑
c. ANS, 4.26↑
d. ANS (Armenak), 4.11↓
355a. *Rev.* of 354d. ANS (Armenak), 4.17↓
b. *Commerce (Asia Minor '61)
c. Commerce (Asia Minor '61)
d. ANS, 4.05↑
e. *Rev.* to r., amphora. ANS, 4.04↑

356a. *ANS (Armenak), 4.20↑
b. *Rev.* to r., amphora. *ANS (Cavalla), 4.09↑
357a. *ANS (*SNGBerry* 266), 4.27↑; Commerce 1970
b.[31] ANS, 4.21↑
c. *Rev.* to r., amphora. *ANS, 4.13↑
d. *Rev.* as 357c. ANS, 4.20↑; ANS, 4.25↑

Series XV, the last issue at Sardes in the names of both Alexander and Philip, is somewhat smaller than the preceding TI emission but similar to it in basic format. Only three control symbols are employed: rose, torch and bee. The first is apparently reserved for Philip's coinage and the others more or less equally shared by the two rulers. On four drachm reverses (355e, 356b and 357c-d) a second symbol, an amphora, appears in the right field while other reverses from the same obverse dies have only the standard markings.

Nike now normally advances left and on some stater dies the full inscription ΒΑΣΙΛΕΩΣ ΑΛΕΞΑΝΔΡΟΥ is again used. Zeus is generally, but not invariably, depicted with crossed legs; occasionally, as in earlier issues, the engraver has taken pains to indicate that the god is sitting on a throne rather than a stool.

One noteworthy aspect of Series XV is the appearance of a stater with the types of Philip II. This is an isolated occurrence, as at Miletus, but whereas the Milesian staters seem to belong to the beginning of the reign of Philip III, those of Sardes date from a few years before his death.

The transfer of five obverse dies (one for staters, one for tetradrachms and three for drachms) links Series XIV and XV.

Series XVI. Control: Α and STAR

Staters

Rev. to l., star; to r., Α

358. *Obv.* of 303. *Rev.* Nike advances r.; to l., inscription; to r., star and Α. *London
359. *Obv.* of 302. *London (Larnaca)
360. *London
361. *Yakountchikoff Coll., 8.27

Tetradrachms

Rev. to l., star; below throne, Α

362. *Rev.* below, Α . *Oxford (*SNG* 3166), 17.10↑
363. *ANS (Mesopot. '20), 16.80↓
364. *ANS, 16.83↓

[31] The area where the amphora would be if it were part of the original die is off flan on this coin.

365a. *ANS, 16.89↑
b. Berlin
c. Hollschek Coll., 17.06
366. *Athens; ANS, 17.05↑
367. *ANS, 16.94↑

Series XVII. Control: Γ, A and STAR

Tetradrachms

Rev. to l., Γ; below throne, A above star

368. *Obv.* of 367
a. *Rev.* star? London
b. ANS (= A. Cahn Mar. 10, 1913, 112), 16.91←
c. *ANS, 17.08↑
369a. *Rev.* no star. Univ. of Chicago
b. Vienna
c. Commerce (Asia Minor '70), 16.78↓
d. *Rev.* no star; to r., amphora. ANS, 17.11↓; Commerce 1919, 16.88
e. *Rev.* to r., amphora. *ANS (= Egger May 2, 1912, 600), 17.02↑
f. *Rev.* as 369e. Stockholm, 17.10↑
g. *Rev.* to l. beside Γ, amphora. *Dattari Coll.
h. *Rev.* as 369g. Hermitage
370. *Rev.* below, leaf replaces star; to r., amphora. *London

Series XVIII. Control: F, A and AMPHORA

Tetradrachms

Rev. to l., F; below, A; to r., amphora

371. *Obv.* of 366. *Rev.*: below, A. *Commerce 1978, 17.05
372. *Obv.* of 369, recut
a. Amer. Univ. Beirut; Paris
b. *Rev.* to l., star above F; no amphora. *London; Private Coll. (Aksaray), 17.07
373. *Rev.* below, A. *Amer. Univ. Beirut
374.[32] *Obv.* of 367. *Rev.* to l., amphora above F. *Vienna
375. *Obv.* of 365. *Rev.* to l., star above F; no amphora. *The Hague
376a. *Rev.* to l., F; below, A above star; no amphora. *G. Hirsch June 28, 1960, 54
b. *Rev.* probably as 376a with star off flan. ANS, 17.07→

[32] On the reverse die of 374 there is an X above the strut of the stool and the same marking appears between the two struts of nos. 377-79. This would seem to be merely a decorative device.

377a. *Rev.* to l., ℲF; below, only tip of A or A visible; no amphora. London
b. *Rev.* to l., star above ℲF; below, A. *The Hague
c. *Rev.* as 377b. London
d. *Rev.* as 377b. Seyrig Coll.
378. *Rev.* to l., leaf above F or ℲF; below, A. *Vienna
379a. *Rev.* of 378. *Athens
b. *Rev.* to l., star above ℲF; below, only tip of A or A visible. Vienna
c. *Rev.* to l., leaf above ℲF; below, only tip of A or A visible. Athens (Pontoleibade-Kilkis), 16.70
d. *Rev.* to l., leaf(?) above ℲF; below, A. ANS, 17.07↓
e. *Rev.* to l., ℲF; below, A above bee; no amphora. Berlin
f. *Rev.* as 379e. *ANS, 17.07↑

Series XIX. Control: ℳ and STAR

Tetradrachms

Rev. to l., star above ℳ

380a. *Rev.* to l., K; below, ℳ. *Berlin. With star cut over K: *Athens (Sparta)
b. Paris, 16.95↑
c. *ANS, 16.88↑
d. Commerce (Asia Minor '70), 16.88↑
e. Commerce (Asia Minor '70), 15.96→
381a. *Malloy Mar. 28, 1973, 142
b. ANS (Mesopot. '20), 16.40→
c. Commerce (Asia Minor '70), 15.59→
d. *Rev.* monogram above star. ANS (Ankara), 17.06←
e. *Rev.* as 381d. Commerce (Asia Minor '70), 16.49↑
382a. *Rev.* of 381e. Cambridge (Grose 3433), 16.98→; Commerce 1956 (Phacous)
b. Myers-Adams Mar. 15, 1973, 80 (= G. Hirsch June 22, 1966, 144)
c. *Rev.* monogram above star. ANS, 16.00↑
d. *Rev.* as 382c. *Vienna
e. *Rev.* as 382c. Petsalis Coll.
383a. *Rev.* of 382e. Athens
b. *ANS, 17.03→
c. The Hague
d. Commerce (Mersin)
384a. *Rev.* of 383d. *ANS, 17.13→; Paris (de Luynes 1630), 17.05
b. Oxford (*SNG* 2840), 16.94↑
c. *Rev.* monogram above star. London; Berlin; Hermitage, 16.85↓
385a. *Rev.* to l., star; below, ℳ. *Copenhagen (*SNG* 859), 16.98↑
b. *Rev.* as 385a. ANS, 16.68↓; Hermitage

386a. *Rev.* monogram above star. *Vienna; Pozzi Coll.; Commerce before 1941
b. *Rev.* as 386a. Athens; The Hague
c. *Rev.* as 386a. ANS, 16.43↑; Spink *Num. Circ.* June 1972, 6154, 16.88
d. *Rev.* as 386a. ANS, 17.05↑
e. *Rev.* as 386a. ANS (Armenak), 16.98→
f. London; Copenhagen (*SNG* 858), 16.97←; Commerce (Asia Minor '70), 16.89↑

Series XX. Control: 𐌼

Staters

387a. *Rev.* to l., star; to r., 𐌼. *London (Larnaca); Private Coll., 8.54↑
b. *Rev.* to l., ®; to r., 𐌼. *Berlin
c. *Rev.* to l., Ⓚ and ®; to r., 𐌼. *Hermitage
388. *Rev.* to l., 𐌼 above Ⓚ. *London
389. *Obv.* griffin on helmet. *Rev.* to l., 𐌼 above Ⓚ and Π below wing. *ANS, 8.54↓; Berlin; Hess-Leu Mar. 27, 1956, 273

Tetradrachms

Rev. to l., star; below, 𐌼

390a. *Munich
b. Berlin
391a. *London
b. ANS, 17.16↑; ANS, 16.80↑
c. Berlin
d. Glasgow (Hunt. 1, p. 301, 52), 16.73
e. ANS, 17.00↓
f. *Rev.* monogram omitted. Commerce (Asia Minor '70), 15.74↑
392. *ANS, 16.92↑

Rev. to l., 𐌼; below, 𐌼

393. *Obv.* of 392. *Private Coll. (Aksaray), 16.32
394. *Obv.* of 391, recut
a. *Rev.* to l., monogram omitted. Cambridge (*SNGLeake* 2144), 16.67→
b. Vienna
c. Commerce 1971, 16.81
d. *Rev.* to l., 𐌼. ANS, 16.53↑
e. *Rev.* to l., 𐌼; below, 𐌼 above amphora. *Athens (Pontoleibade-Kilkis)

Rev. to l., ⍑; below, 𐌼

395. *Vienna

Rev. to l., [monogram] ; below, [monogram]

396a. *ANS, 17.04↑
b. *Rev.* to l., [monogram] . ANS, 16.85↑
397a. Commerce (Asia Minor '70), 16.47↑
b. *Rev.* to r. between stool and scepter, I. *London
c. *Rev.* as 397b. Athens; ANS, 16.94←

Drachms

Rev. to l., [monogram] ; below, [monogram]

398a. *ANS (Armenak), 4.13→
b. ANS (Armenak), 4.21→
c. ANS, 4.16→
d. Munich, ←; Paris
399. *ANS (Armenak), 4.11↑
400a. ANS (Cavalla), 4.08→
b. *ANS (Armenak), 4.16↑
401. *Rev.* of 400b. *Dresden, 4.09
402. *Rev.* to l., probably [monogram] ; below, Δ above [monogram]. *ANS (Armenak), 4.15↓
403a. *ANS (Cavalla), 4.18←
b. Gans Apr. 19, 1960, 251 (= Naville 1, Apr. 4, 1921, 941), 4.23

Obv. recut

c. *Rev.* below, Δ above [monogram]. Athens (Megara)
d. *Rev.* as 403c. London

Rev. to l., [monogram] ; below, [monogram]

404. *ANS, 4.28↓
405a. *ANS (Armenak), 4.24↑
b. ANS (Armenak), 4.15↓; Athens (Megara)
c. ANS (Larissa), 4.18↓; ANS (Armenak), 4.12↑
d. ANS (Armenak), 4.25↓
e. ANS, 4.18↑
f. ANS (Armenak), 4.14↑
g. ANS (Armenak), 4.06↑; Oxford (*SNG* 2841), 4.21↓
h. Munich
i. London

Bronze Unit

Obv. Shield with caduceus in center

Rev. BA and helmet; to l., caduceus; below, [monogram]; to r., rose

406. *ANS, 3.12↑

Series XXI. Control: [monogram]

Tetradrachms

407. *Rev.* to l., [monogram] ; below, A. *ANS (Armenak) 16.89←

408. *Obv.* of 407. *Rev.* to l., [monogram] above forepart of lion; below, [monogram]. *ANS (Armenak), 16.96→; ANS, 16.79→

Series XXII. Control: [monogram]

Stater

409. *Rev.* ΒΑΣΙΛΕΩΣ ΛΥΣΙΜΑΧΟΥ; to l., forepart of lion above [monogram]; to r., [monogram]. *Hirsch May 11, 1911, 443 (= Hirsch Nov. 29, 1909, 248), 8.44 (holed)

Tetradrachms

Rev. ΒΑΣΙΛΕΩΣ ΛΥΣΙΜΑΧΟΥ; to l., forepart of lion; below, [monogram]

410a. *Rev.* ΑΛΕΞΑΝΔΡΟΥ; to l., [monogram] above forepart of lion. *London

b. *Rev.* to l., [monogram] below forepart of lion. ANS (*SNGBerry* 430), 16.93↑

c. *Rev.* as 410b. *London (= Weber 2718), 17.07; Berlin; ANS, 16.83↑

Obv. recut

d. *Rev.* as 410b. Cambridge (*SNGLeake* 1837), 16.59↑

e. *Rev.* as 410b. ANS (= Münz. u. Med. FPL 98, Dec. 1950, 8), 16.92↑; Munich; London

Series XXIII. Control: [monogram] and [monogram]

Stater

411. *Obv.* of 409. *Rev.* ΒΑΣΙΛΕΩΣ ΛΥΣΙΜΑΧΟΥ; to l., forepart of lion and [monogram] ; to r., [monogram]. *ANS, 8.52↑

Tetradrachms

412. *Rev.* ΒΑΣΙΛΕΩΣ ΛΥΣΙΜΑΧΟΥ; to l., [monogram] above forepart of lion; below, [monogram]. *ANS (= Florange-Ciani Feb. 17, 1925, 319), 17.03↑; London; Paris

The final fourth-century issues of Alexandrine money at Sardes present problems in chronology and arrangement similar in some degree to those which marked the beginning of the coinage. That Series XVI-XX belong together is evident from the plates and from the pattern of die transfers outlined in the catalogue; that they are related to the first emissions of Lysimachus (Series XXI-XXIII) rather than the last strikings of the Philip III period (Series XIV-XV) seems to me equally clear. One must, I believe, postulate a temporary cessation of coinage, paralleling the situation at Miletus, but of shorter duration.

While it is true that there is a carry-over of two stater obverses (nos. 358-59) from the A issue to that with A and star, there is nothing inherently improbable in the assumption that the mint in closing down c. 318 kept its well-preserved obverse dies for possible future use and that two of these, and perhaps others of which we have no record, were put back into service when coinage was resumed. Certainly the abnormal reverse coupled with one of the dies, which shows Nike advancing right instead of left and without stylis, is more likely to have been produced in the initial stages of a mint reorganization than in the context of an established and ongoing coinage.

Otherwise there is no ostensible connection between the present issues and those of the earlier period. This is now basically a tetradrachm coinage with some gold but very few drachms. The Heracles heads of the large silver are engraved in higher relief, the profiles are heavier even to the point of coarseness, and the locks of the lion's mane are rendered with greater freedom and boldness. In general the obverses of the drachms display a similar pattern. One notes, however, that even in the final stages of coinage, there are occasional echoes of earlier stylistic conventions. Drachm reverses alternate between a Zeus with spread legs and one with legs crossed. Nike is normally shown in motion but three stater dies, two from the time of Lysimachus, revert to the static pose. On one obverse die Athena's helmet is adorned with a griffin in place of a serpent.

When the mint reopens after a hiatus of some years, it adopts a control system which is essentially new but has some links with the past. The first issue adds a star to the A which had been employed in Series XV, but no subsidiary symbols are used. The star continues to be a part of the basic control for the next four emissions although there are a number or instances in which it is omitted or replaced by other markings, which are familiar from earlier strikings. Series XVII and XVIII are die-linked to Series XVI in a pattern which makes it difficult to tell in what order they appear, if indeed they are not concurrent issues.

A-Star	Γ-A-Star	F-A-Amphora
367 —	— 368 —	— 374
	369 —	— 372
365 —	—	— 375
366 —	—	— 371

An amphora, which was part of the control on four drachm dies of Series XV, appears on some reverses of both the Γ-A and F-A strikings, and a leaf is occasionally associated with the same two emissions. A bee replaces the amphora on two reverses of Series XVIII.

Series XIX is less complicated, controlled consistently by star and [monogram], a monogram which was encountered earlier at Sardes. For a time, too, Series XX uses only star and monogram but the symbol is soon replaced by a variety of secondary monograms, usually within a circle, a convention that carries over into the coinage of Lysimachus (Series XXI-XXIII).[33]

SYNOPSIS OF THE COINAGE

	Staters[a]			*Tetradrachms*			*Drachms*			*Bronze*		
	No. coins	*Obv. dies*	*Rev. dies*	*No. coins*	*Obv. dies*	*Rev. dies*	*No. coins*	*Obv. dies*	*Rev. dies*	*No. coins*	*Obv. dies*	*Rev. dies*
I: Ram's hd.	5	2	2									
II: Stag's hd.	14	3	2									
III: Serpent	25	10	10									
IV: Griffin's hd.	20	9	8				2	1	1			
V: Tripod	11	7	4									
VI: Bucranium	16	5	5	1	1	1	2	1	1			
VII: Cantharus							8	4	6			
VIII: Mithras hd.	3	2	2	2	1	1	3	3	3	2	2	2
IX: [monogram]	1	1	1	1	1	1	53	19	41	3	3	3
X: |⊙|	4	2	2				74[b]	43	65			
XI: NK	2	1	1				41	24	33			
XII: [monogram]	5	3	4				31	20	27			
XIII: [monogram]	15	6	8				78	36	58	3	3	3
XIV: TI	38	12	23	30	11	26	153	50	96	2	2	2
XV: A	18	8	11	14	6	9	120	46	95			
XVI: A-Star	4	4	4	9	6	8						
XVII: Γ-A-Star				13	3	12						
XVIII: F-A-Amphora				21	9	18						
XIX: [monogram]-Star				42	7	27						
XX: [monogram]	8	3	5	23	6	21	27	8	22	1	1	1
XXI: [circled monogram]				3	1	2						
XXII: [monogram]	1	1	1	9	1	5						
XXIII: [circled monogram]-[monogram]	1	1	1	3	1	1						
TOTALS[c]	191	80	94	171	54	132	592	255	448	11	11	11

[a] The count includes 1 distater and 8 fractions.

[b] Including 1 triobol.

[c] The carry-over of obverse dies from one issue to another reduces the totals by 21 for staters (of which 15 involve Series I-VI), 6 for tetradrachms and 13 for drachms.

[33] Of the six entries associated with Lysimachus (nos. 407-412) four are published in M. Thompson, "The Mints of Lysimachus," *Essays in Greek Coinage Presented to Stanley Robinson* (Oxford, 1968), p. 172, nos. 78-81.

The excavations at Sardes have turned up a fair number of bronzes from the time of Alexander and the Successors with Heracles head/bow and club and shield/helmet types, but for the most part symbols and monograms are illegible. It is interesting to note, however, that several bronzes with the name and types of Lysimachus have the unusual [circled monogram] marking of our Series XXI. See T. V. Buttrey, et al, *Greek, Roman and Islamic Coins from Sardis* (Cambridge, Mass., 1981), pp. 16-18.

CHRONOLOGY

In all probability Sardes was the first of the Asia Minor drachm mints to coin for Alexander. This is not surprising. The capture of Sardes surely held special significance for Alexander since this was not merely another "liberated" city but a center of Persian power. Furthermore and of even greater importance, the acquisition of the royal Persian mint must have provided a substantial amount of coinage and bullion for Alexander's treasury. When the time came to begin minting operations in Asia Minor beyond the Taurus, Sardes would have been a logical first choice.[34]

For a few years the mint's output consisted of gold alone and indeed, prior to 325 B.C., the bulk of the stater coinage of Asia Minor came from Sardes.[35] Once silver coinage commenced on a large scale, the amount of gold declined substantially although there is a marked upturn for a few issues after 321 B.C.[36]

Apart from some scanty emissions associated with Series IV-VIII there is practically no silver until Series IX. Drachms are then produced in abundance through Series XV. Series XIV-XV also include a substantial number of tetradrachms and from that point on the coinage is basically large silver. Five issues of bronze can be identified.

Various hoards provide a framework for the chronology. Saida (*IGCH* 1508) and Asia Minor 1964 (*IGCH* 1437) would seem to have been buried at about the same time, c. 321/0 B.C. In both deposits the Sardes material stops with Series XIII.[37] There is no later coinage in Demanhur (*IGCH* 1664), dated c. 318, and this is rather puzzling since Series XIV includes a sizable issue of tetradrachms and is die-linked with Series XIII.[38] In the slightly later Sinan Pascha Hoard of 317/6 B.C. (*IGCH* 1395), Series XIV and XV are well represented and they are in the Paeonia Hoard of c. 315 (*IGCH* 410).

Between 315 and 305, the one hoard of relevant material which has a secure burial date is the large Abu Hommos find of c. 311/0 according to Newell (*IGCH* 1667). There is no Sardian coinage later than Series XV with the name of Philip III. In hoards interred c. 300, however, the late Sardes issues appear.[39] A few tetradrachms of Series

[34] A central location and established communication facilities would have been additional reasons for opening a mint there.

[35] Some gold issues from Magnesia seem to have been struck before 325 but they are comparatively small emissions. From other mints there is nothing.

[36] The record of known dies for the coins of Sardes is outlined on p. 40.

[37] The record goes no further than Series II in Asia Minor 1950 (*IGCH* 1442), which can only be a few years earlier in date, but this is a small hoard with a heavy concentration of south Anatolian and Phoenician issues.

[38] In Newell's publication there is nothing from either Series XIV or XV, but a recent article by Orestes Zervos ("Additions to the Demanhur Hoard of Alexander Tetradrachms," *NC* 1980, pp. 185-88) includes one coin of Series XV: rose and A in the name of Philip III. If this piece is indeed from the hoard, then the absence of TI tetradrachms is all the stranger. For a possible explanation, see p. 86.

[39] It is the tetradrachm hoards that are most significant since the only drachms of the late period are those of Series XX and they are not numerous.

XVII-XX turn up in Aksaray (*IGCH* 1400), Phacous (*IGCH* 1678) and Mosul 1862 (*IGCH* 1756). Larnaca (*IGCH* 1472) contained a stater of Series XVI and another of Series XX.

The crucial hoard is that of Aleppo (*IGCH* 1516) which had at least 27 examples of Series XVI-XIX, all in fine to mint condition according to Newell's record with those of Series XIX the most numerous and the best-preserved. If, as seems likely, the deposit was laid away c. 300 or slightly later, the Sardian tetradrachms must belong to the last decade of the fourth century.

Taking the evidence as a whole, the chronological pattern that emerges can be outlined as follows:[40]

Series	Symbol	Date
I:	Ram's hd.	c. 330-325
II:	Stag's hd.	
III:	Serpent	
IV:	Griffin's hd.	
V:	Tripod	
VI:	Bucranium	
VII:	Cantharus	
VIII:	Mithras hd.	
IX:	[monogram]	c. 325/4
X:	[monogram]	c. 324/3
XI:	NK	c. 323/2
XII:	[monogram]	c. 322/1
XIII:	[monogram]	c. 321/0
XIV:	TI	c. 320/9
XV:	A	c. 319/8
XVI:	A-Star	c. 310-302
XVII:	Γ-A-Star	
XVIII:	F-A-Amphora	
XIX:	[monogram]-Star	
XX:	[monogram]	
XXI:	[monogram]	c. 300/9 (Lysimachus)
XXII:	[monogram]	c. 299/8 (Lysimachus)
XXIII:	[monogram]-[monogram]	c. 298/7 (Lysimachus)

[40] Bracketing to the left indicates die-linkage.

MILETUS

ATTRIBUTION

Identification of Miletus as one of Alexander's major drachm mints rests upon firm grounds. As Newell has demonstrated,[41] the city struck coinage for Demetrius Poliorcetes during the initial decade of the third century. After Ipsus, which gave Lysimachus theoretical control of western Asia Minor, Demetrius managed to retain his hold on Caria [42] and it was at Miletus that he issued gold and silver of the Alexander type, first with the name of Alexander and then with his own. The last emission, inscribed ΔΗΜΗΤΡΙΟΥ, is die-linked to a striking with the ΜΙ monogram of the Milesian autonomous coinage, thus establishing Miletus as the mint of the Demetrius sequence.

The bipennis, a Carian symbol par excellence, is prominently featured on the staters, tetradrachms and drachms which belong to the time of Demetrius. The same symbol appears on the gold and on some bronzes of earlier date and although the associated large and small silver normally lacks the double-axe marking, identity of basic controls and extensive die-linkage prove that a single mint is involved.

Only the first Milesian emission stands apart in that it makes no use of the bipennis symbol and is not connected by die transfer to any other issue. As will be apparent from the plates, however, the engraver who produced some of the obverses and reverses for its gold was clearly the same man who cut dies for the next issues on which the bipennis is displayed.

CATALOGUE AND COMMENTARIES

Series I. Control: ΜΙ

Staters

Obv. below neck, fulmen

Rev. to l., monogram; to r., inscription

1. *Alexandria
2. *ANS, 8.56↑; London

[41] *Demetrius*, pp. 59-63.

[42] In this he was undoubtedly aided by his alliance with Seleucus and by Lysimachus's preoccupation with affairs elsewhere as well as by his father's enlightened policy toward the Greek cities when most of Asia Minor was under Antigonid control.

3a. *Rev.* of 2. ANS cast (Topolovo); Franceschi FPL 1968, 8 (= Franceschi FPL 1967, 6)
b. *ANS, 8.59↑; London, 8.62; Schlessinger Feb. 4, 1935, 664 (= Egger 41, Nov. 18, 1912, 381), 8.59; Stacks Sept. 6, 1973, 254 (= Stacks Apr. 30, 1964, 9), 8.56
4. *Rev.* of 3b. *London (Svoronos, *Ptolemies*, pl. 1, 2), 8.50; Glasgow, 8.55
5. *Stockholm (Saida), 8.60↑
6a. Münz. u. Med. FPL 318, Nov. 1970, 8, 8.53
b. *Saroglos Coll. (= Santamaria Apr. 6, 1908, 235), 8.60; Commerce (No. Greece '66), 8.52; Hollschek Coll., 8.55; Coin Galleries Nov. 22, 1963, 299; Sotheby Mar. 9, 1936, 187; Harlan Berk FPL 2, Fall 1974, 50, 8.57
c. London; Helbing Apr. 9, 1913, 292
7a. *Rev.* of 6c. *Kricheldorf July 1, 1966, 65 (Asia Minor '64)
b. Ball 6, Feb. 9, 1932, 155, 8.50
8a. *Rev.* of 7b. *Naville 6, Jan. 28, 1924, 715, 8.59; Florence; Hermitage (from barrow of Great Blisnitza on Taman Peninsula), 8.57↗; Ciani Dec. 12, 1921, 18; Oxford (*SNG* 2774), 8.61↑
b. Vienna, 8.52↑
c. Paris (Delepierre 972); Gans Apr. 19, 1960, 234
9a. *Commerce (Asia Minor '50); Hermitage
b. Portland (Oregon) Art Museum; Coin Galleries FPL 6, 1962, F4; Vinchon Oct. 29, 1973, 16
10. *Obv.* fulmen? *Commerce (No. Greece '66), 8.52
11. *ANS, 8.58↗; Coin Galleries Apr. 20, 1961, 4
12a. *Rev.* to lower r., monogram. *ANS (*SNGBerry* 161), 8.59↗; ANS (Saida?), 8.53↑; Bourgey June 24, 1975, 10, 8.49
b. *Rev.* as 12a. Ratto Apr. 4, 1927, 575 (= Ratto FPL Dec. 1922, 1950), 8.60
13. *Obv.* no fulmen. *Istanbul, 8.62↑
14. *Obv.* as 13. *ANS, 8.49↑; Münz. u. Med. FPL 327, Sept. 1971, 23, 8.55
15. *Obv.* fulmen? *Rev.* to lower l., monogram. *Berlin, 8.58↑

Half Stater

Obv. as above

Rev. as 15

16. *ANS (*ANSMN* 12, p. 13), 4.26↓

Quarter Staters

Obv. as above

Rev. as 15

17. *London (= Weber Coll. 2079), 2.15; Paris, 2.16↑

Staters

Obv. as above

Rev. as 15

18a. Berlin (Abusir), 8.60↑
b. *ANS (Saida ?), 8.58↑
c. London (Larnaca)
19a. *Rev.* of 18c. Commerce (Asia Minor '50)
b. Cahn 84, Nov. 29, 1933, 245, 8.22
c. *Rev.* to lower r., monogram; to l., circular inscription. *Athens

Distaters

Obv. as above

Rev. as 19c

20. *Athens (Svoronos, *Ptolemies*, pl. 1, 1) 17.20↗; Berlin, 17.14↑

Staters

Obv. no fulmen

Rev. as 19c

21a. *ANS, 8.63↑; Berlin
b. Vienna; ANS cast (Topolovo), 8.58↑; Hermitage, 7.95 (very worn)↑; Coin Galleries Mar. 23, 1971, 110 (= Stacks June 1940, 646), 8.58; London (Larnaca).

Philip II Staters

Rev. below horses, ΙΑΡ

22. *London
23. *London; The Hague; Berlin; ANS, 8.59↑

Tetradrachms

Rev. to l., monogram; below throne, fulmen

24a. *Rev.* positions of symbol and monogram reversed. *ANS, 17.11↑
b. *Rev.* as 24a. ANS (Demanhur; *Reattrib.*, pl. 29, 10), 17.21↑
25. *Berlin, 16.41↑; Berlin (Svoronos, *Ptolemies*, pl. 1, 3), 16.97↑
26. *ANS, 17.20↑
27a. *London; ANS (Abu Hommos), 17.11↑
b. ANS, 17.21↑; Commerce (Demanhur; *ANSNNM* 19, pl. 4, 3)

Eagle Drachms

Rev. to r., monogram

28a. *Seyrig Coll. 1971, 4.17↑
b. London

29a. *ANS, 4.25↑ (= Kress Oct. 23, 1963, 376)
b. ANS (*SNGBerry* 250), 4.10↑
30a. *London
b. Oxford (*SNG* 2517), 4.22↑
31. *Hermitage

Drachms

Rev. to l., fulmen; below throne, monogram

32. *Obv.* of 31?
a. *ANS (Sinan), 4.23↑; ANS, 3.82↑
b. ANS, 4.21↑
33. *ANS (Sinan), 4.23↑
34. *ANS (Sinan), 4.22↑; ANS (Cavalla), 4.19↑
35a. Cambridge (*SNGLeake* 2227), 3.99↑
b. Rauch June 4. 1971, 32, 4.30
36. Berlin, 4.24↑; Commerce 1970
37. Ratto Apr. 4, 1927, 677, 4.28
38. ANS (Sinan), 3.58↑
39a. ANS, 4.26↑
b. *ANS (Mosul '17), 4.11↑
40. *ANS, 4.18↑
41. ANS (Sinan), 4.26↖
42 *ANS, 4.13↑
43a. ANS, 4.24↑
b. Oxford (*SNG* 2780), 4.19↖
44. *Rev.* of 43b. Berlin, 4.11↑
45. ANS (Sinan), 4.29↑
46. *ANS, 4.01↑
47a. ANS (Sinan), 4.25↑; ANS (Sinan), 4.22↑
b. ANS (Sinan), 4.21↑
48. *ANS (Armenak), 4.10↑
49. ANS, 4.13↑
50. *ANS (Sinan), 4.26↑
51. Commerce (Asia Minor '61), 4.22↑
52. Berlin, 4.23↑
53. *Turin, 4.17↑

Rev. to l., monogram; below throne, star

54a. *ANS (Sinan), 4.16↑
b. ANS (Cavalla), 4.13↑; Helbing Oct. 24, 1927, 2844, 4.30; Commerce (Thessaly)
c. Berlin

Rev. to l., monogram

55. *ANS, 4.25↗
56a. ANS, 3.96↑
b. Oxford (*SNG* 2775), 4.15↑
57a. *ANS (Cavalla), 4.17↓
b. Cambridge (*SNGLeake* 2230), 4.26↑
58. Egger 40, May 2, 1912, 744
59. Helbing Jan. 31, 1930, 202, 4.50
60. Ratto Apr. 4, 1927, 693, 4.24
61. ANS (Sinan), 4.11↑
62. Cambridge (*SNGLeake* 2228), 4.00↓
63. ANS (Sinan), 4.25↑
64. ANS, 4.18↑
65. Yale Univ. (Bab)
66. *ANS, 4.32↑; Aberdeen (*SNGDavis* 149), 4.19↑
67. ANS (Sinan), 4.25↑
68a. ANS, 4.29↑
b. *von Post Coll., 4.26↑; Commerce 1970
69. ANS, 3.95↑
70. Hersh Coll. (Asia Minor '64), 4.30↑
71. ANS (Sinan), 4.29↑
72. *ANS (Armenak), 4.25↑; ANS, 4.16↑
73. *ANS (Sinan), 4.26↑; ANS, 4.12↑
74. *Stockholm, 4.14↑
75. Bettermann Coll.
76a. *Cambridge (*SNGLeake* 2229), 4.30↑
b. ANS (Sinan), 4.28↑
77. ANS, 4.24↑
78a. ANS (Cavalla), 4.23↑
b. ANS (Sinan), 4.28↑; Athens (Corinth), 4.08
c. ANS (Sinan), 4.24↑
d. ANS, 4.16↑
e. ANS, 4.14↑
79. ANS (Sinan), 3.85↑; G. Hirsch May 28, 1962, 98
80. *ANS (Sinan), 4.22↑; ANS (Cavalla), 4.25↑
81. ANS (Sinan), 4.30↑
82a. *ANS (Sinan), 4.27↑
b. ANS (*SNGBerry* 251), 4.14↑
c. Commerce (Asia Minor '61); Oxford (*SNG* 2776), 4.25↑
83. ANS, 4.20↑
84a. *Commerce (Asia Minor '64)
b. Oxford (*SNG* 2777), 4.07↗

c. ANS, 3.90↗
d. ANS, 3.86↗
85. *ANS, 4.16↗
86a. ANS (Sinan), 4.24↑
b. *Commerce (Asia Minor '64)
87. Oxford (*SNG* 2778), 4.14↗
88. ANS (Sinan), 4.27↗
89. *ANS (Sinan), 4.24↑; ANS (Sinan), 4.26↑
90a. *ANS (Sinan), 4.28↑; ANS (Sinan), 4.30↑
b. ANS (Sinan), 4.29↑; ANS, 4.14↑
91a. *ANS (Sinan), 4.28↗; Commerce (Asia Minor '64)
b. ANS (Sinan), 4.27↗
92a. *ANS (Sinan), 4.32↑
b. ANS (Sinan), 4.25↗; ANS, 4.19↗
93. Seltman Coll.
94a. ANS, 4.11↗
b. Commerce (Asia Minor '64)
95. ANS (Cavalla), 4.15↑; Turin, 4.21↑
96. Yale Univ. (Bab)
97. *ANS (Sinan), 4.20↑
98. ANS (Sinan), 4.27↑
99a. ANS, 4.08↑
b. ANS (Sinan), 4.22↑
100a. *ANS (Sinan), 4.27↑
b. ANS (Sinan), 4.28↑; ANS (Sinan), 4.25↑
c. ANS (Sinan), 4.27↑; ANS (Sinan), 4.29↑
101. *ANS, 4.28↗
102. ANS (Siphnos), 3.93↓
103a. *ANS (Sinan), 4.24↗; Commerce (Asia Minor '64)
b. ANS (Sinan), 4.28↑
c. ANS (Sinan), 4.22↗
d. ANS (Sinan), 4.23↗
104. ANS, 4.17↑
105a. ANS, 4.05↗
b. ANS, 4.05↑
106a. *ANS, 4.21↑; ANS (Cavalla), 4.24↑
b. Zygman Coll.
107a. ANS (Larissa), 4.10↑
b. ANS (Cavalla), 4.18↓
c. Berry Coll., 4.15
108. Hersh Coll. (Asia Minor '64), 4.31↑
109a. *ANS (Sinan), 4.30↑
b. ANS (Sinan), 4.23↑; Benson Coll., 4.16↑; Malloy FPL 19, Oct.-Nov. 1970, 403

110a. Münz. u. Med. FPL 247, Sept. 1964, 12 (Asia Minor '64), 4.26
b. *Commerce (Asia Minor '64)
111a. *ANS (Armenak), 4.23↗
b. ANS (Cavalla), 4.13↑
c. Commerce 1970
112. *ANS (Sinan), 4.27↑; ANS, 4.13↑
113a. *ANS (Sinan), 4.34↑
b. ANS (Sinan), 4.30↑
c. ANS, 4.26↑
d. ANS, 4.08↑
114. *ANS (Sinan), 4.22↑
115. Commerce (Asia Minor '61), 4.15↓
116a. *ANS (Sinan), 4.23↑; ANS (Armenak), 4.02↑; Hersh Coll. (Asia Minor '64), 4.29↑
b. Glasgow, 4.22; Kress Apr. 2, 1973, 190
117. London
118a. *ANS (Sinan), 4.27↑
b. ANS (Larissa), 4.17↑
119. Kress Oct. 28, 1960, 310, 4.20
120. *ANS (Cavalla), 4.13↑
121. *ANS (Sinan), 4.27↑
122. ANS (*SNGBerry* 252), 4.32↑
123. *ANS (Sinan), 4.31↑

This first issue of Alexanders at Miletus is by far the most extensive of the series with as many obverse dies as are recorded for the remainder of the coinage at that mint. Both gold and silver have distinctive aspects. The Alexander gold was produced in four denominations: a sizable output of staters supplemented by small issues of half and quarter staters as well as distaters, the last an excessively rare denomination outside of Macedonia. Almost all obverses are marked with a small fulmen below the neck of Athena, thus providing the same combination of symbol and monogram that is found on the tetradrachms and some of the associated drachms.

Diversity in obverse style and reverse format is noteworthy. The heads of the earlier staters are rather large; the hair falls loosely with two long locks curling forward and back over the neck while the inner terminal of the crest crosses the outer at the nape and swings upward. On later dies the two loose curls are omitted and the hair hangs limply or is twisted into corkscrew curls. Crest terminals are often rendered in zigzag fashion and the heads are smaller.

On the reverses Nike stands stiffly, holding a long stylis. Her hair is rolled back from her face and normally arranged in a chignon on the top of her head with a confining ribbon clearly visible on some dies. Monogram and inscription shift position within the issue. The former appears in the center of the left field on the earlier dies and then drops to lower left or lower right, below the wing. The name of Alexander, which generally reads straight down in the right field, is later moved to the left field to read upward in a curved line, an arrangement which carries over into the next issues.[43]

Doubles and fractions are to be associated with late rather than early stater dies: nos. 16 and 17 are strikingly similar to no. 15 while no. 20 is an enlarged version of no. 19. The emission of posthumous Philip staters, employing at least two pairs of dies, is almost certainly to be considered part of this issue despite the variation in monogram. That the coins were struck in Asia Minor is evident from the fact that the obverse of no. 23 was later used with a Magnesia reverse showing a bee and spearhead below the horses. This phenomenon of die linkage between mints, involving Philip staters, will be discussed in connection with the coinage of the Ionian mints.

Some tetradrachms and a very great many drachms constitute the remainder of the issue, All reverses of the large silver and a substantial number of those cut for fractions are marked with both monogram and fulmen symbol. The latter is replaced briefly by a star on the reverses of no. 54; other drachms have the monogram alone in the left field. In sheer size this initial emission of drachms at Miletus is overwhelming and may well prove to be the largest single issue of drachms at any of Alexander's Asia Minor mints. Nearly 100 obverse dies are on record and one can be quite certain that originally many more were employed since a high proportion of entries are known from only one example. As a coinage of this magnitude, even if spread over several years, would have required a number of die cutters, it is not surprising that one finds considerable variation in both obverse and reverse representations.

What is surprising, however, is the appearance at Miletus of two kinds of drachms: the standard type and also the eagle on fulmen variety otherwise attested for the mint of Amphipolis alone. The eagles seem to have been produced in small quantity but four obverse dies are known, one of which was probably used with a standard reverse.[44]

Series II. Control: ΓΡ

Staters

Rev. to l., inscription; to r., bipennis; to lower r., monogram

124a. *Rev.* ¶Π. *London

b. *Rev.* of 124a with monogram recut: ¶Π changed to ΓΡ. *ANS, 8.57↑; Berlin; Grunthal Dec. 5, 1949, 368

[43] This placement of the legend is rare but it does occur sporadically elsewhere. See p. 13 and n. 17 above for examples at Sardes, Sidon and Ake. Newell (*Sidon and Ake*, p. 25) suggests that the intent was to show Nike crowning Alexander's name in tribute to the great victory at Issus.

[44] The Hermitage piece (no. 31) is in such poor condition that certainty is impossible, but I feel fairly confident that the obverse of no. 32 is the same die with some recutting probable. In any event the same hand is involved.

Series III. Control: EAR OF BARLEY

Staters

Rev. to l., inscription; to r., barley; to lower r., bipennis

125. *Rev.* positions of symbols reversed. *ANS (= Sotheby May 4, 1908, 303), 8.56↑
126. *Rev.* of 125. *ANS (Larnaca = Ratto Apr. 4, 1927, 572 = Naville 5, June 18, 1923, 1394), 8.54↑; Berlin; Commerce (Asia Minor '50)
127a. *Berlin; ANS, 8.56↑; Münz. Basel Mar. 15, 1938, 206, 8.57; Bucharest Inst. Arch. (Gîldău), 8.45; Commerce 1920 (Saida?)
b. Hess-Leu Apr. 7, 1960, 145, 8.57↑; ANS, 8.09↑; Coin Galleries Apr. 19, 1962, 1 (Asia Minor '50)
c. Paris (Delepierre Coll. 973)
128. *ANS, 8.16↗; Berlin; Glasgow (Hunt. 1, p. 297, 20), 8.55; Athens; Hermitage; London; Paris; Copenhagen (*SNG* 633), 8.57↑; Münz. u. Med. FPL 162, Nov. 1956, 4
129. *Rev.* to r., inscription; to lower r., bipennis; to lower l., barley. *London; Hermitage (Anadol), 8.54↑; Berlin; Copenhagen (*SNG* 632), 8.50↑ Egger 39, Jan. 15, 1912, 263; Commerce (No. Greece '66), 8.49; Münz. u. Med. FPL 187, Feb. 1959, 2; Ratto FPL Dec. 1922, 1946; Kastner Nov. 26, 1974, 26, 8.55; Münz. u. Med. 41, June 18, 1970, 74, 8.58

Quarter Staters

Rev. to r., inscription; to lower r., barley; to l., bipennis

130. *London; Naville 5, June 18, 1923, 1406, 2.11; Helbing 70, Dec. 9, 1932, 581 (= Riechmann 30, Dec. 11, 1924, 447), 2.12; Münz. u. Med. FPL 353, Feb. 1974, 21, 2.11
131. *Commerce 1928, 2.09↗
132. *ANS (= Hirsch 12, Nov. 17, 1904, 114), 2.06↑; Copenhagen (*SNG* 656), 2.08↑

Tetradrachms[45]

Rev. to l., barley

133. *Commerce 1955
134a. ANS (Demanhur), 17.16↑
b. *ANS, 17.16↑; ANS, 17.15↑; Commerce (Asia Minor '70), 15.80↗; Commerce before 1941
135. *Rev.* of 134b. *ANS, 17.14↑

[45] Only four entries in the catalogue can definitely be identified as coming from Demanhur but it is likely that a number of other tetradrachms, acquired by the ANS from the Endicott and Storrs Collections, were originally from that find.

136a. *ANS, 17.14↑; ANS, 17.11↑; Grabow 14, July 27, 1939, 257; Coin Galleries Nov. 20, 1975, 1450, 17.17
b. ANS, 17.18↑; Commerce before 1941
c. ANS, 17.10↑
137a. *Toronto (Demanhur), 17.12; ANS, 17.16↑; ANS, 17.15↑; Naville 1, Apr. 4, 1921, 898, 17.11; Schlessinger Feb. 4, 1935, 703, 17.20
b. ANS ("Tripolitsa"), 17.14↑; Brussels (de Hirsch 1063), 17.07↑
c. ANS, 17.16↑; Commerce (Manissa), 17.06
d. *Obv.* die recut during its use with this reverse. *ANS, 17.11↗; ANS, 17.26↑
e. ANS, 17.16↗; ANS (Demanhur; *Reattrib.*, pl. 18, 9), 17.20↗; Egger 40, May 2, 1912, 628
f. ANS, 17.05↑
138. *Oxford (Demanhur; *SNG* 2783), 17.09↑

Drachms

Rev. as above

139a. *Commerce (Asia Minor '64)
b. ANS (Cavalla), 4.13↑; ANS, 4.07↑
140a. *ANS (Sinan), 4.26↗
b. von Post Coll., 4.09↑
141. *Rev.* of 140b. Athens, 3.95↑
142. *ANS, 4.24↑; ANS, 4.18↑
143. *Rev.* of 142. *Cambridge (*SNGLeake* 2191), 4.14↗
144. *ANS, 4.23↑
145. *ANS (Cavalla), 4.16↑; Copenhagen (*SNG* 877), 4.14↑
146. *ANS, 4.06↑
147. *ANS, 4.19↑; G. Hirsch Oct. 3, 1961, 1512

Hemidrachms

Rev. as above

148a. *Commerce, date uncertain
b. Münz. u. Med. FPL 296, Jan. 1969, 7

Bronze Units

Rev. below club, ear of barley

149. *ANS, 5.90→
150a. ANS, 5.49→
b. ANS, 5.59→
151. *ANS, 6.81→
152. *ANS, 6.03→
153. ANS, 5.74→
154. ANS, 6.08→
155. *ANS, 5.42→
156. *ANS (found at Physcus), 5.52→

Series II, comprising a few staters from a single pair of dies, seems to have been a short-lived experiment, quickly replaced by Series III. That the gold with ΓΡ comes between that of Series I and III is clear from a comparison of obverse and reverse dies. The Athena head of no. 124 is remarkably close, especially in the treatment of hair and crest terminals, to nos. 18-20 and also to nos. 125-27. On the reverse the basic formula of circular legend in the left field and monogram to lower right carries over from nos. 19-21 but a bipennis has now been added center right. The reverse of nos. 125-26 shows an identical arrangement with an ear of barley taking the place of the monogram. Later reverses of the gold are less consistent: the inscription moves from left to right field on nos. 129-32; the ear of barley on the staters shifts from lower right to center right and finally to lower left; the bipennis appears center left on nos. 130-32 but is placed to lower right on nos. 127-29, the position it will retain through Series VIII.

The output of tetradrachms is roughly equivalent to that of Series I but there is substantially less fractional silver, with the result that one finds a general stylistic homogeneity that is lacking in Series I. Bronze units of Alexander type with the ear of barley symbol form a part of this issue. That the Milesian attribution is correct is apparent from the marked similarity of Heracles heads on silver and bronze.[46] The provenance of no. 156, from the coastal town of Physcus in Caria, is confirmatory evidence.

It is noteworthy that the bipennis, which is a characteristic feature of the gold throughout the remainder of the coinage, is not placed on the silver and bronze until considerably later. Bronze coins of Series VII and VIII carry the symbol but it is not added to the silver until Series IX.[47]

Series IV. Control: FULMEN

Stater

Rev. to l., fulmen; to lower r., bipennis

157. *ANS, 8.51↖

Series V. Control: [monogram]

Tetradrachms

Rev. below throne, monogram

158a. Vienna (= Egger 40, May 2, 1912, 638), 17.14↗
b. *Helbing Mar. 20, 1928, 186 (= Naville 10, June 15, 1925, 443 = Naville 1, Apr. 4, 1921, 902), 17.10

[46] Compare nos. 134 and 149, nos. 147 and 151-52.

[47] The sole recorded exception is no. 215 of Series VIII.

c. Vienna (Aleppo), 17.05↗; Vienna, 16.98↗; ANS (Demanhur, *ANSNNM* 19, pl. 4, 4), 17.16↗
d. Commerce 1975
e. Bourgey Mar. 27, 1912, 158
f. Oxford (Kuft; *SNG* 2781), 17.03↗; Oxford (*SNG* 2782), 17.05↗
159a. *Rev.* of 158f. *Naville 1, Apr. 4, 1921, 903, 17.06
b. ANS, 16.58↑
c. Naville 1, Apr. 4, 1921, 904, 17.19; H. H. King Coll.
d. ANS, 17.13↗
e. *Glendining Oct. 3. 1973, 11

Series VI. Controls:  and 

Tetradrachms

Rev. to l., first monogram; below throne, second monogram

160. *Obv.* of 159. *ANS (Demanhur; *Reattrib.*, pl. 18, 10), 17.15↑; Haughton Coll. (Demanhur; Sotheby Apr. 30, 1958, 53), 17.15↑
161a. *ANS, 17.17↑
b. ANS, 17.22↑; Alexandria
162a. ANS (Abu Hommos), 17.12↑
b. *Obv.* die slightly recut at this stage. ANS, 17.13↑; Morgenthau Nov. 26, 1934, 193; Beirut Natl. Mus.
c. H. M. F. Schulman Nov. 25, 1967, 825 (= Münz. u. Med. June 17, 1954, 1107 = Ratto Apr. 4, 1927, 663), 17.10
d. *Naville 1, Apr. 4, 1921, 926, 17.22
163a. *Rev.* of 162d. ANS, 17.18↑
b. ANS, 17.18↑
c. *Athens; ANS, 17.14↑
164a. *Rev.* of 163c. ANS, 17.09↑
b. *ANS, 17.08↑
165a. *ANS (Abu Hommos), 16.40↑; London
b. ANS (= Egger 40, May 2, 1912, 581), 16.99↑

Bronze Units

Rev. below club, 

166. *ANS, 5.60→
167. *ANS, 5.89→
168. *ANS, 5.11→

With Series IV we have another isolated issue of gold, this time known from a single stater. Although its exact position in the sequence connot be determined, it seems to belong with either Series V or VI. The presence of the bipennis separates it from Series I, the only other issue to use a fulmen symbol, while the position of the inscription and symbols would apparently rule out an association with Series II or the early dies of Series III. In style the charming Athena head with its delicate features and formal curls is very similar to no. 128 of Series III and almost equally close to no. 169 of Series VII. The scale of the bipennis is perhaps significant. When it first appears on the reverses of nos. 124-27, the axe is a prominent adjunct to the type; subsequently it is greatly reduced in size and inconspicuously tucked away under Nike's left wing. Compare the representations on nos. 128-29, 157 and all staters of Series VII.

Series V involves a small issue of tetradrachms from two obverse dies. The ten recorded reverses are of particular interest in their representation of the type. In this issue alone Zeus sits on a high-backed throne instead of the usual stool and his pose is remarkable for its rigidity. On earlier tetradrachm dies the god is generally portrayed with legs uncrossed but slightly spread, giving an impression of relaxation; in Series V the legs are held close together in uncompromising stiffness.[48] Toward the end of the issue, on reverses 159d and e, one notes a rearrangement of Zeus's drapery. The thick fold of cloth swathing the lower torso has been loosened to allow a fold to fall below the seat of the stool, a rendering which appears on all later tetradrachm dies.

Series VI is linked to Series V by a shared obverse die. A break above the two lowest locks of the lion's mane, starting as a mere hairline on some coins of no. 159 and becoming more pronounced on both examples of no. 160, establishes the sequence of issues. Five additional obverse dies are recorded for Series VI but, as in the case of Series V, no fractional silver is associated with the tetradrachms.

An emission of bronze is attributed to Series VI, in accordance with Newell's arrangement of his trays, although the connection cannot be considered absolutely certain. The Heracles heads are not dissimilar to those of the tetradrachms, allowing for the difference in scale, but there is not the close stylistic affinity so apparent in the drachms and bronze of Series III. The reverses of nos. 166-68 are, however, identical with those of the earlier striking: bow in case with opening to left above and club to right below the name of Alexander. Furthermore, the die orientation of the two lots of bronze is consistently fixed at three o' clock. Given the degree of variation within the type as a whole,[49] this parallelism is a persuasive argument for linking the two issues as the output of a single mint.

The monogram below the club, although it contains elements of both tetradrachm monograms, is not identical with either. Drachms of Series X do have exactly the same marking but they belong to the time of Demetrius Poliorcetes, who had his own bronze types and is unlikely to have reverted to those of Alexander.

[48] The only exception is no. 159e, obviously the work of a different engraver whose cross-legged Zeus, like those of Series VI, has lost his throne but regained his ease.

[49] The club, facing either left or right, is sometimes above and sometimes below the name. Similarly the bow in case shifts position and orientation; frequently it is replaced by a bow and quiver. Die axes vary considerably. At Lampsacus, for example, where the club is above the name, the dies are fixed at nine o'clock; at Sardes, where the placement of the weapons corresponds with Milesian practice, the dies are loose: ↓ ← ↖ ↑

Series VII. Control: KH

Staters

Rev. to l., monogram; to lower r., bipennis

169a. *Rev.*: monogram omitted. *ANS, 8.56↑
b. *Rev.* KH. *ANS, 8.52↑
c. *Rev.* as 169b. Helbing Nov. 8, 1928, 3835, 8.50
d. Helbing Oct. 24, 1927, 2828, 8.60
170a. Hermitage; Berlin (Larnaca)
b. Kricheldorf July 1, 1966, 64; G. Hirsch Apr. 2, 1959, 779
c. *Paris; Coin Galleries FPL 1, 1963, A2; Gibbons FPL 8, Autumn 1975, 16 (= Glendining Dec. 11, 1974, 20)
171a. *Rev.* of 170c. Hermitage
b. *ANS (= Naville 15, July 2, 1930, 480 = Hirsch 34, May 5, 1914, 292), 8.62↑
c. Frank. Münz. 12, Apr. 1966, 5
172. *London
173. *ANS (*SNGBerry* 162), 8.59↑; Gotha; Glasgow (Hunt, 1, p. 298, 32), 8.53; Hermitage; Paris (de Luynes 1611), 8.60; Commerce 1921; Hess-Leu Apr. 7, 1960, 144
174a. *ANS (= Naville 1, Apr. 4, 1921, 868), 8.56↑
b. ANS cast (Topolovo)
175a. *Saroglos Coll.; Hermitage; Saroglos Coll.
b. Commerce (Paeonia), 8.51↑
176a. *Rev.*: bipennis omitted. Zelensky Barrow, Taman Peninsula (*Arch. Anz.* 1913, p. 180), 8.49↑
b. *Hess 208, Dec. 14, 1931, 268 (Anadol); ANS cast (Topolovo)
c. Hermitage (Anadol); Commerce 1921; Myers Dec. 5, 1974, 66, 8.41; Helbing Oct. 24, 1927, 2829, 8.50
177. *Münz. Basel 10, Mar. 16, 1938, 205 (= Münz. Basel 4, Oct. 1, 1935, 629), 8.50

Half Stater

Rev. as above

178. *Paris, 4.28↑

Quarter Staters

Rev. as above

179. *Munich; Athens; Paris, 2.08↑
180. *London

Tetradrachms

Rev. to l., monogram

181. *Obv.* of 165
  a. ANS (Abu Hommos), 17.12↑; ANS (Abu Hommos), 16.40↑; Locker Lampson Coll. 163, 17.04; Copenhagen (*SNG* 747), 17.18↑
  b. ANS, 17.05↑; Empedocles Coll.
  c. London
  d. Oxford (Demanhur; *SNG* 2784), 17.28↑; Oxford (Kuft; *SNG* 2785), 17.10↑; Münz. u. Med. 19, June 5, 1959, 397; ANS (Abu Hommos), 16.67↑; ANS, 16.87↑
  e. ANS (Abu Hommos), 17.12↑
  f. Münz. u. Med. FPL 327, Sept. 1971, 21; ANS (Abu Hommos), 13.31 (pl)↑
  g. *ANS, 16.97↑

182a. *ANS (Demanhur; *Reattrib.*, pl. 18, 11), 17.16↗
  b. London; Oxford (Kuft; *SNG* 2788), 17.04↗
  c. Oxford (Kuft; *SNG* 2789), 17.14↗

183a. *Rev.* of 182c. ANS, 16.98↑; Hermitage
  b. *Rev.*: ΗΙ. *ANS, 17.15↑; ANS (Demanhur, *Reattrib.*, pl. 18, 12), 17.17↑; ANS, 17.11↑; Haughton Coll. (Demanhur; Sotheby Apr. 30, 1958, 52), 17.22↗; English priv. coll., 17.22↗
  c. Oxford (Kuft?; *SNG* 2787), 17.23↑
  d. Dewing Coll. (= Naville 6, Jan. 28, 1924, 752), 17.15
  e. Oxford (Demanhur; *SNG* 2786), 17.17
  f. ANS, 16.41 (broken)↑
  g. ANS, 17.11↗

184. *ANS, 17.16↑; Peus June 20, 1960, 781 (= Naville 6, Jan. 28, 1924, 729), 17.17

Drachms

Rev. as above

185a. ANS (Sinan), 4.25↑
  b. *ANS (Sinan), 4.30↑; ANS, 3.97↑
  c. ANS (Sinan), 4.26↑

186. *ANS (Sinan), 4.28↑

187. *ANS (Cavalla), 4.20↑

188. *ANS (Sinan), 4.27↑

189. *ANS (Sinan), 4.29↑

190. *ANS, 4.07↑

191a. ANS (Sinan), 4.29↑
  b. *ANS (Sinan), 4.32↗; ANS (Sinan), 4.32↗

192. *Rev.* of 191b. *ANS (Sinan), 4.26↑; ANS (Sinan), 4.26↑

193a. *ANS (Sinan), 4.19↑; ANS, 3.79↑
  b. Yale Univ. (Bab)

194a. *ANS (Sinan), 4.30↗; ANS (Armenak), 4.20↗
b. ANS, 4.07↑
195a. ANS (Sinan), 4.13↑
b. ANS (Sinan), 4.16↑
196. *ANS, 4.05↑
197. *ANS, 4.26↑

Bronze Units (Philip)

Rev. above horseman, bipennis; below, monogram

198. *ANS, 5.71←
199. *ANS, 4.87←
200. *ANS, 5.32←
201. *ANS, 5.44←
202. *ANS, 5.14←
203. ANS, 4.90←

After a period of limited production, the mint of Miletus becomes more active with Series VII. Output, although considerably lower than that of Series I, is closely comparable with that of Series III, both in quantity and in the range of metals and denominations.

Once again we have a substantial amount of gold, involving fractions as well as staters. Obverses dies, similar in style, are in the tradition of nos. 128-29 and 157, but the reverses display a new and distinctive element. In earlier issues the stylis which Nike holds is rendered as a plain cross bar bisected by a shaft with a bulbous terminal.[50] On the reverses of the present emission tiny Nikes adorn the ends of the cross bars.[51] Newell, noting the same decorative motif on early Sidonian staters, suggested an allusion to naval victories in connection with the siege of Tyre.[52]

Linkage between issues is once more provided by a tetradrachm die: no. 165 of Series VI carries over to no. 181 of Series VII. Two die breaks, extending down from the lowest lock of the lion's mane, are more prominent when the obverse is used with KH reverses. Tetradrachms and drachms show a strong stylistic affinity and would seem to be the work of the engraver who produced the tetradrachms of Series VI.

Bronze was also issued but now the types are those of Philip II: Apollo head and horseman galloping to the right with ΒΑΣΙΛΕΩΣ ΦΙΛΙΠΠΟΥ above and below the rider. The presence of both bipennis and monogram is unusual; heretofore the symbol has been reserved for gold emissions.

[50] See no. 128 for a particularly clear example.

[51] When the top of the standard is on flan, the minute figures are always visible; sometimes very sketchily drawn but usually quite recognizable as on nos. 171b, 175 and 178.

[52] Newell, *Sidon and Ake*, pp. 7, 25.

Series VIII. Control: W

Staters

Rev. to l., monogram; to lower r., bipennis

204. *Obv.* of 177. *ANS (*SNGBerry* 163), 8.48↑; London
205. *Berlin (Topolovo?)
206. *Rev.* of 205. *ANS, 8.60↑

Tetradrachm

Rev. to l., monogram

207. *Hersh Coll., 17.22

Drachms

Rev. as above

208. *ANS, 4.24↑
209. *ANS (Armenak), 4.22↑; ANS (Armenak), 4.19↑
210. *ANS (Armenak), 4.14↑; Athens
211. *Obv.* of 209
  a. *Rev.* below throne, Ⓜ. *ANS (Sinan), 4.05↑
  b. *Rev.* as 211a. ANS (Armenak), 4.21↑
212. *Obv.* of 210
  a. *Rev.* below throne, ME. *ANS (Armenak), 4.20↑
  b. *Rev.* as 212a. Athens
213a. *Rev.* as 212a. *ANS, 4.21↑; ANS (Larissa), 4.05↑
  b. *Rev.* as 212a. ANS (Armenak), 4.08↑
  c. *Rev.* as 212a. ANS, 4.07↑; Paris; Stockholm, 4.07↑; London
214. *Rev.* below throne, A cut over ME within wreath: (ME). *Hermitage
215. *Rev.* to l., W above bipennis. *Athens
216. *Obv.* of 215. *Rev.* no markings. *ANS (Cavalla), 4.07←; Athens

Bronze Quarter (Philip)

Rev. above horseman, monogram

217. *ANS, 1.19←

Bronze Units (Alexander)

Rev. above horseman, bipennis and W; below, ME

218. *ANS, 3.83←
219. *ANS, 3.99←
220. *Rev.* ctmk: fulmen. *ANS, 4.13←
221. *Rev.* bipennis? *ANS, 4.34←
222. *Rev.* below, (ME). *ANS, 5.20←
223. *Rev.* obscure; ctmk: fulmen. *ANS, 3.30←

IMITATION?

Stater

Rev. to l., bipennis above ME

224. *ANS (Mărăşeşti), 8.11↑

One obverse die of Series VII continues to be used for the first staters of Series VIII, thus linking the issues. A pronounced die break across the lower crest terminals, present on no. 204 but not visible on no. 177, fixes the sequence. The few dies known for the gold of the present striking are similar in style to those of the preceding series, and again small Nikes decorate the cross bar of the stylis.

Only one tetradrachm is on record, clearly from the hand of the engraver who produced nos. 181-84 in the KH sequence. The more abundant small silver shows evidence of confusion or disturbance at the mint. Although early obverses are of respectable style, there is a marked deterioration in the workmanship of nos. 214-15. The first reverses conform to the normal pattern of monogram or symbol in the left field; subsequently supplementary monograms appear below the throne (nos. 211-14). On no. 215 the second monogram has been dropped and a bipennis added to the left field; while another reverse coupled with a later state of the same obverse die has no markings.

Bronze is struck in two denominations with diverse legends. A single quarter unit carries the W monogram and the name of Philip; units with the same types but stamped with basic monogram, bipennis and secondary monogram bear the name of Alexander. A fulmen, which had been used as an adjunct device or symbol on earlier Milesian issues, now appears as a countermark on some of the larger bronzes.

Presumably to be connected in some way with Series VIII is a strange stater from the Mărăşeşti Hoard (no. 224). The Athena head is fairly well executed but the Nike of the reverse is little better than a caricature: coarse features, exaggerated "pony-tail" hairdo and misunderstood stylis (⌐'). The iconspicuous bipennis of preceding issues has been shifted from lower right field to a position of prominence below Nike's outstretched arm in association with the ME monogram found on some small silver and bronze. There is no trace of the basic control monogram and the weight is very low. Since Series VIII is abnormal in other respects, no. 224 may be an official striking but on the whole it seems more likely that it represents an imitation from the Danubian area, perhaps a poor copy of an unrecorded issue.

With Series VIII the coinage of Alexander types at Miletus comes to a temporary halt. Apparently the mint was inactive during the remainder of the century, with production resumed only after Ipsus.

Series IX. Control: HELMET CREST

Staters

Rev. to l., crest; to lower l., bipennis

225. *ANS (Mărăşeşti), 8.44↑; Paris; Hermitage (Anadol)
226. *Rev.* of 225. *Berlin
227. *Rev.* Nike carries palm. *ANS (Anadol = Hess 208, Dec. 14, 1931, 289), 8.42↑; The Hague; Hermitage
228. *Rev.* as 227. *London; Paris

Drachms

Rev. to l., crest; below throne, bipennis

229a. *Rev.* symbols transposed. *ANS 4.22↑
b. *Rev.* as 229a. ANS (Armenak), 4.17↑
230. *Rev.* as 229a. ANS (*SNGBerry* 253), 4.12↑
231a. *ANS (Larissa), 4.22↑
b. ANS (Cavalla), 4.14↑; Commerce 1971, 4.13
232a. *ANS, 4.27↑; ANS (Armenak), 4.19↑
b. ANS, 4.18↑
c. ANS, 4.22↑; ANS, 4.24↑
d. ANS, 4.26↑
233a. *ANS, 4.26↑
b. Athens (Corinth), 4.18
c. Rome, Terme
234. ANS (Cavalla), 4.12↑
235. ANS, 4.19↑
236. *ANS (Cavalla), 4.22↑
237a. *ANS (Armenak), 4.24↑; ANS (Armenak), 4.21↑
b. Paris; Yale Univ. (Bab)
238. *ANS, 4.27↑

In the publication of the Bab Hoard,[53] Series IX was isolated from the rest of the Milesian coinage and dated c. 310 B.C. At the time there seemed no clear evidence for a connection with either the earlier or later issues of that mint. Since then two new coins (nos. 238 and 242) have appeared, providing die links between the helmet crest striking and the early third century money of Demetrius Poliorcetes. The obverse die of no. 228 is used for staters of Series XII while the obverse of no. 238 is shared by drachms of Series X.

[53] See n. 1 above.

Even without this proof of contemporaneity, there is good reason to associate Series IX with Series X-XIII. On the reverses of the gold, the bipennis, which had invariably been placed in the lower right field on all but the earliest issues, is moved to the left, below Nike's wing in Series IX and to center field thereafter. More significantly, Nike at times carries a palm branch instead of the customary stylis. One reverse die of Series IX has the stylis and two the palm; in Series XII there is one stylis and one palm; all four reverses of Series XIII as well as that of the subsequent ꟿ staters (Plate 31, A) show the palm. Prior to Series IX the bipennis symbol had been reserved for the gold.[54] In Series IX-XIII it appears on large and small silver as well.

Series X. Control: ꟿ

Drachms

Rev. to l., monogram; below throne, bipennis

239. *Obv.* of 238. *ANS, 4.28↑; ANS (Armenak), 4.05↑; Berlin; Petsalis Coll., 4.16
240. *Rev.* of 239. *ANS (Armenak), 4.24↑; Saroglos Coll.

Series XI. Control: ⓔ

Tetradrachms

Rev. to l., monogram; below throne, bipennis

241a. *Berlin
b. London; Saroglos Coll. (= Egger 40 May 2, 1912, 630)
c. ANS, 16.58↑; Paris

Series XII. Control: Ꮲ

Staters

Rev. to l., monogram above bipennis

242. *Obv.* of 228. *Rev.* Ꮲ. *Commerce 1971, 8.46
243. *Rev.* of 242. *Berlin
244. *Rev.* Nike carries palm. *Berlin; Brussels (= Hess-Leu 24, Apr. 16, 1964, 141), 8.45

[54] Except for one drachm of Series VIII, no. 215, and the bronze issues of Series VII and VIII.

Tetradrachms

Rev. to l., monogram; below throne, bipennis

245. *Commerce (Asia Minor '70), 16.43↖
246a. ANS, 16.86↑; Copenhagen (*SNG* 748), 15.64↑
b. London; Grabow July 9, 1930, 294, 16.75; ANS (Armenak), 16.82↑
c. *Münz. u. Med. June 18, 1970, 83
247a. *Rev.* of 246b. Berlin; Commerce (Asia Minor '70), 16.71↗
b. *Rev.* of 246c. ANS, 16.53↑; Berlin; Natl. Mus. Lebanon
c. *ANS, 16.96↑
d. Athens; Athens (Corinth), 16.85
e. London
f. Commerce (Mersin)
248a. Milan; Paris; Commerce (Asia Minor '70), 16.75↑
b. Yale Univ., 17.13↑
c. *ANS (Zemun), 16.90↑
d. Berlin
249a. *ANS, 16.99↑; Commerce (Asia Minor '70), 15.66↗
b. Athens; Hollschek Coll., 17.07
c. ANS, 16.91↑; Commerce (Karaman), 16.11
d. Mass. Hist. Soc.; Amer. Univ. Beirut; Commerce (Asia Minor '70), 16.33↗
e. Commerce (Asia Minor '70), 16.61↘
250a. *Cambridge (*SNGLeake* 2301), 17.00↑
b. Mass. Hist. Soc.
251. *Athens (Epidaurus)
252a. *Morgenthau May 9, 1935, 134, 16.91↑
b. Paris
c. Commerce (Mersin)

Drachms

Rev. as above

253. *Obv.* of 240. *ANS (Armenak), 4.22↑; ANS, 4.26↑
254. *Rev.* of 253. *ANS, 4.12↑
255. Yale Univ. (Bab)

Series XIII. Control: ⊛

Staters

Rev. to l., monogram above bipennis

256. *Obv.* of 244. *Rev.* Nike carries palm. *London; Sotheby Feb. 27, 1908, 48
257. *Rev.* of 256. *ANS (*Demetrius*, pl. 4, 17), 8.52↑
258a. *Rev.* as 256. *ANS, 8.35↑
b. *Rev.* as 256. Hermitage (Anadol)
c. *Rev.* as 256. Athens (*Demetrius*, pl. 4, 18)

Tetradrachm

Rev. to l., monogram; below throne, bipennis

259. *Berlin (*Demetrius*, pl. 4, 19), 17.01↑

Drachms

Rev. as above

260a. *ANS (Larissa), 4.20↑
b. Oxford (*SNG* 2792), 4.20↖; Cambridge (*SNGLeake* 2302), 4.17↖; Cambridge (Grose 3497), 4.08↑
261a. ANS (*SNGBerry* 254), 4.32↑; ANS, 4.21↑; Lockett Coll. (*SNG* 1482), 4.28↑
b. Helbing Dec. 9, 1932, 588
262a. ANS (Armenak), 4.18↑; ANS, 4.05↑
b. *ANS (Larissa), 4.18↑
c. ANS, 4.15↑
d. Copenhagen (*SNG* 896), 4.12↑
263a. *ANS (Armenak), 4.25↑
b. Naville 6, Jan. 28, 1924, 767, 4.17
264a. ANS, 4.10↑
b. *Washington, U.S. Mint
265a. *ANS (Mosul '17), 4.18↑
b. ANS, 4.18↑
266. ANS, 4.11↑; Merzbacher Nov. 15, 1910, 403 (= Ratto Apr. 26, 1909, 1926)
267. *ANS, 4.01↑
268. ANS (*Demetrius*, pl. 4, 20), 4.20↑
269. *Dewing Coll.
270. ANS, 4.04↑
271. ANS (*SNGBerry* 255), 4.26↑
272. *Knobloch Coll.

The association of Series X-XIII is confirmed not only by style but by a gratifying sequence of die links. As noted above, the issue with helmet crest symbol (Series IX) shares an obverse drachm die with Series X, and the latter in turn passes along one of its drachm obverses to Series XII (nos. 240 and 253). Stater dies are also transferred. There is apparently no gold coinage for Series X and XI; when staters are again struck in Series XII an old obverse from Series IX is used (nos. 228 and 242). Another stater die is shifted from Series XII to Series XIII (nos. 244 and 256) and, finally, as Newell points out,[55] Series XIII shares a stater obverse with an issue of autonomous coinage bearing the ΜΗ monogram (nos. 258 and A on Plate 31).

[55] *Demetrius*, p. 61.

Two of the four series seem to have been small emissions: Series X represented by a few drachms and Series XI by a few tetradrachms struck from the same obverse die. The next two issues on the other hand have the full complement of staters, tetradrachms and drachms although the silver output of Series XII is chiefly tetradrachms and that of Series XIII almost exclusively drachms.[56] In view of the disparity in size, it would be hazardous to regard all four series as annual emissions. A year's output is probable in the case of Series XII-XIII, less likely for Series X-XI. All strikings, however, must belong to the general period c. 300-294 B.C. when Demetrius Poliorcetes controlled Miletus. Within this time frame the order of issuance is certain with the sole exception of Series XI, an unlinked coinage containing only tetradrachms. The style of its obverse die seems closer to nos. 245-46 of Series XII than to any other obverses of the sequence, but this is not definitive evidence for placement.

SYNOPSIS OF THE COINAGE

	Staters[a]			*Tetradrachms*			*Drachms*			*Bronze*[b]		
	No. coins	*Obv. dies*	*Rev. dies*	*No. coins*	*Obv. dies*	*Rev. dies*	*No. coins*	*Obv. dies*	*Rev. dies*	*No. coins*	*Obv. dies*	*Rev. dies*
I: [monogram]	70	23	31	9	4	6	173	95	142			
II: [monogram]	4	1	1									
III: Barley	39	8	9	30	6	13	17[c]	10	11	9	8	9
IV: Fulmen	1	1	1									
V: [monogram]				15	2	10						
VI: [monogram] - [monogram]				20	6	12				3	3	3
VII: [monogram]	41	12	22	34	4	17	24	13	18	6	6	6
VIII: [monogram]	4	3	2	1	1	1	20	6	13	7[d]	7	7
IX: Crest	9	4	3				23	10	18			
X: [monogram]							6	2	1			
XI: [monogram]				5	1	3						
XII: [monogram]	4	3	2	39	8	23	4	3	2			
XIII: [monogram]	6	3	2	1	1	1	27	13	21			
TOTALS[e]	178	58	73	154	33	86	294	152	226	25	24	25

[a] The count includes 2 distaters and 15 fractions.

[b] Bronzes of shield/helmet type with bipennis and K controls (Plate 31, B and C) are probably Carian issues under Demetrius. Miletus may be the mint but this is far from certain.

[c] Including 2 hemidrachms.

[d] Including 1 bronze quarter unit.

[e] The carry-over of obverse dies from one issue to another reduces the totals by 3 for staters, 2 for tetradrachms and 2 for drachms.

[56] Seven other drachms listed by Newell (*Demetrius*, p. 61) can be added to the present catalogue—six in Berlin and one in Paris.

CHRONOLOGY

Unlike the other drachm mints of Asia Minor, Miletus struck no gold or silver in the name of Philip III, and thus we are deprived of a valuable chronological peg. There are, however, three issues with the types of Philip II—one gold and two bronze—which can be assigned to the years of the joint kingship of Philip III and the young Alexander IV; these would seem to be Miletus's sole gesture in recognition of the dual reign.

For the rest we are dependent on the hoards, of which five provide the basic evidence. Even so there is a measure of uncertainty in that the output of Miletus is unbalanced. As the synopsis on p. 65 shows, there are issues without staters and drachms; their absence from one hoard or another can have no significance.

Two gold hoards, Saida (*IGCH* 1508) and Asia Minor '50 (*IGCH* 1442), and one fractional silver deposit, Asia Minor '64 (*IGCH* 1437), are roughly contemporary in their burial date of c. 320 B.C. or slightly earlier. These hoards contained staters and drachms with ΜΙ, ΓΡ, and barley ear controls. The condition of the coins is excellent; they cannot have circulated long before interment. A single issue of Philip II staters has the ΜΙΡ monogram, which is surely a more elaborate version of the ΜΙ found on staters, tetradrachms and drachms of Miletus's initial emission. If, as Le Rider argues,[57] the posthumous staters of Philip II began, after a six year interval, to be produced again in Macedonia and if the situation in Asia Minor is analogous, as it seems to be,[58] then this striking at Miletus would belong to the final months of 324/3 B.C. The ΜΙ emission is a very large one, the most extensive by far of any Milesian issue, and probably covered more than a single year. It may well have begun c. 325 when other Asia Minor mints initiated or increased production, for whatever reason, and lasted until the dual reign was established. During Alexander's lifetime, then, there would have been a more or less uniform coinage with ΜΙ and two subsidiary controls. After his death a more elaborate system was introduced with controls changing annually and the distinctive bipennis added to the gold strikings.

Demanhur (*IGCH* 1664), with a firm burial date c. 318 B.C., includies the ΜΙ and barley ear issues as well as the die-linked strikings of Series V-VII.[59] This last has associated bronzes with the types of Philip II and the ΒΑΣΙΛΕΩΣ ΦΙΛΙΓΓΟΥ inscription, which one may interpret as a reference to Philip III. One gold stater of Series VII comes from the Paeonia Hoard of c. 315 (*IGCH* 410).

57 *Philippe*, pp. 429-38.

58 As noted below (p. 84 and n. 77), the emission of Philip II staters in Asia Minor may have started a year or two later than 324 B.C., the date suggested for several mints in the publication of the Bab Hoard (*IGCH* 1534). For further discussion of these staters and a possible explanation of their reappearance c. 323/2, see M. Thompson: "Posthumous Philip II Staters of Asia Minor," *Festschrift* in honour of Paul Naster (forthcoming).

59 Newell records 68 tetradrachms, unequivocally attributed to Miletus, as coming from this hoard. All specimens except those with ΜΙ are described as in very fine to brilliant condition.

In Sinan Pascha (*IGCH* 1395), interred c. 317/6, all early drachm issues are represented, at least through KH and probably through W as well. One well-preserved piece of that issue, no. 211a, was with the hoard coins and its ticket carried the same "Athens Find" label as other Sinan specimens which had been purchased in Athens, but the "Find" had been crossed over and hence there is some question as to provenance. In any case a die transfer links Series VIII to Series VII and a single bronze with the Philip II types and legend provides additional evidence for dating the W issue to the time of Philip III.

After this there is no coinage at Miletus until the very end of the century. In hoards buried between 315 and 300,[60] only the strikings of 325-318 are present.

Following the disastrous defeat at Ipsus, Demetrius Poliorcetes fled to Ephesus and then to Greece.[61] Shortly thereafter, he was back in southern Asia Minor, landing in Cilicia and taking possession from Pleistarchus, who had been given the province after Ipsus. At Kyinda, c. 299/8, the remains of its great treasure, some 1200 talents, fell into Demetrius's hands, and this bullion likely provided the sinews of a new coinage at Miletus and elsewhere. In *Demetrius*, Newell assigns issues to Salamis, Tarsus, Ephesus and Miletus c. 300-295. Evidently Demetrius was securely in control of the area during those years. In 294 Cyprus was captured by Ptolemy and Demetrius's major mint in that part of the world was lost. How much longer he managed to maintain a foothold in the region is uncertain. The important naval station at Caunus was still in his hands in 286 and the year preceding had witnessed his marriage to Ptolemaïs in Miletus itself. As Haussoullier points out,[62] this would have been impossible if Demetrius's arch-enemy Lysimachus had been in control of the city. Between 294 and 287, however, Demetrius's major mints were those of Amphipolis and Pella in Macedonia where his rule was secure, and it seems probable that the loss of Cyprus, underlining the precariousness of his position in southern Anatolia, resulted in the closing of other royal mints still operating there.

Series IX through XIII would then have been issued during the five or six years when Demetrius held Miletus.[63] The elaborate pattern of die-linkage establishes the sequence but as noted above (pp. 64-65), it is perhaps unwise to try to divide the output by years. All that one can safely say is that the five series were struck c. 300-294 B.C.

In the chronological outline that follows, die-linkage is indicated by brackets to the left.

[60] These include Larnaca (*IGCH* 1472), Abu Hommos (*IGCH* 1667), Kuft (*IGCH* 1670) and Asia Minor '61 (*IGCH* 1444).

[61] The sequence of events is that of Plutarch (*Demetrius* 30-32 and 46). Diodorus (21.4b) says Demetrius went to Cilicia and then to Cyprus.

[62] B. Haussoullier, *Études sur l'histoire de Milet et du Didymeion* (Paris, 1902), p. 30.

[63] These issues are often found in hoards buried c. 285-280 B.C.: Kiouleler (*IGCH* 144), Epidaurus (*IGCH* 158), Thessalonica (*IGCH* 444), Gravena (*IGCH* 148), and Asia Minor '70 (*Coin Hoards* 1, 55).

Series	Date
I: [monogram]	c. 325-323
II: [monogram]	c. 323/2
III: Ear of barley	c. 323/2
IV: Fulmen	c. 322/1
V: [monogram]	c. 322/1
VI: [monogram] - [monogram]	c. 321/0
VII: [monogram]	c. 320/19
VIII: [monogram]	c. 319/8
IX: Crest	c. 300-294
X: [monogram]	c. 300-294
XI: [monogram]	c. 300-294
XII: [monogram]	c. 300-294
XIII: [monogram]	c. 300-294
[monogram]	

HOARDS

As one would expect, there are a great many deposits recorded as having coins of Philip II, Alexander III and Philip III. In the *Inventory of Greek Coin Hoards* nearly 400 entries follow the name of Alexander alone and even when one eliminates bronze hoards and those without material from our Asia Minor mints, one is left with a formidable residue of finds.

Hoards of gold and of silver have been segregated and are presented here in roughly chronological order of burial. Whenever possible their contents are associated with individual coins in the catalogues for Miletus and Sardes. Specific identifications for the other mints await their final publication. With few exceptions, the deposits are included in *IGCH* and references cited there are normally not repeated. Any pertinent publication appearing after *IGCH* was in print is recorded. Of these, the most important is the comprehensive study of Georges Le Rider, *Le monnayage d'argent et d'or de Philippe II.*

ALPHABETICAL LISTING

GOLD HOARDS

Asia Minor 1950 (*IGCH* 1442)
Plate 32

This small hoard of 24 Alexander staters was offered to the ANS in 1950. Nine coins were acquired by purchase or gift and a photographic record was made.

Amphipolis

1-2. Fulmen

Miletus

3-4. ꟿ (T. 9a, 19a)
5-6. Ear of barley, bipennis (T. 126, 127b)

Sardes

7. Ram's head above shell (T. 2)
8-11. Stag's head (T. 3a, 3a, 3b, 5)

Tarsus

12. Plow, ram's head (same obv. die as Newell, *Tarsos*, 18-19)

Citium

13. ꝁ (*SNGBerry* 170; same dies as Newell, *NC* 1915, p. 301, 1)

Salamis

14-18. Eagle[64]

[64] Three of the coins are in the ANS collection: nos. 15 (8.60↑), 17 (8.59↑) and 18 (8.60↑). No one of the five obverse dies is included by Newell in his Cypriote study ("Some Cypriote Alexanders," *NC* 1915, pp. 306-16 but nos. 14-15 share obverses with coins in his collection labelled "Salamis." No. 16 is from the same pair of dies as Svoronos, *Ptolemies*, suppl. pl. A, 2, while no. 18 has the same die combination as Svoronos, *Ptolemies* pl. 2, 3. In the *NC* article Newell differentiates between his one example of a stater with eagle symbol (p. 307, 3) and "much more common ones from another mint" with reference to Svoronos pl. 2, 1-3. That he later changed his mind is evident from his notebook on Cyprus, which postdates the published article. There on the first page of his Salamis section, under the heading "Apparently Salamis in Cyprus," he lists the two Svoronos pieces and also his specimens which share obverse dies with our nos. 14-15. These all precede the Salaminian issues recorded in the *NC*.

Sidon

19. Caduceus (same obv. die as Newell, *Sidon and Ake*, 2H)
20. Club (same dies as Newell 4)

21-22. Star (no. 21 has the obv. die of Newell 5; (no. 22 is an ANS coin, 8.54↑)

Alexandria

23. No marking (*SNGBerry* 186)

Babylon

24. [monogram], H (doublestruck)

The burial date in *IGCH*, c. 310 B.C. is almost certainly based on the Babylonian stater (no. 24) from an issue which Nancy Waggoner assigns to c. 316 and later. That the coin may be an intrusion is suggested by the consistently earlier chronology of the other issues. The Cypriote pieces belong to the first years of Newell's 332-320 period; the Sidonian staters are assigned by him to "late 333 -c. 330 B.C."; the Tarsus coin is dated 327-324 B.C. Although no detailed analysis of the Amphipolis sequence has been made, nos. 1-2 were certainly produced during Alexander's lifetime as was the Alexandrian stater (no. 23) according to Orestes Zervos who is making a mint study of that coinage. Both issues of Sardes and one of Miletus may be attributed to the years before 323, while the second Milesian issue was probably struck shortly thereafter. Its two coins (nos. 5-6) are among the best-preserved specimens in the lot, superior in condition to the Babylonian stater. If this last piece be discounted as intrusive, a burial date for the hoard c. 322/1 B.C. is highly likely. Although the coins appeared on the Istanbul market, their findspot may well have been southern Anatolia, to judge from the representation of mints, and their interment connected with the troubled situation in that part of the world after Alexander's death.

Saida (*IGCH* 1508)

From the sources cited in the *IGCH* the Alexander issues of five Asia Minor Mints can be identified with plausibility although comparatively few coins can be linked with the present catalogues.

Miletus

[monogram] (T. 5; 12a ?, 18b ?)
ΠP, bipennis (Sotheby June 1862, 259 "bipennis and monogram of Priene Π PI)
Ear of barley, bipennis (T. 127a ?)

Sardes

Stag's head
Serpent
Griffin's head
Tripod

Bucranium (T. 33 ?)
[monogram], Mithras head
[monogram], antler (identified as an acrostolion in the catalogue)

Since there is considerable uncertainty as to the exact composition of this hoard or hoards, the burial date is problematical. Newell (*Sidon and Ake*, pp. 57-60), commenting on the absence of issues of Philip III and the fresh condition of the latest Alexander staters of Sidon and Ake, struck in 324/3 B.C., places its interment at about that time.

If one takes into account only the Alexander material, the record is consistent with a burial soon after Alexander's death but perhaps closer to 320 than to 324. One stater of Babylon is later by a number of years and may be intrusive. An issue of Salamis with rudder symbol is dated by Newell c. 320-317 although he notes that it may have begun a few years earlier.[65] The Milesian staters with [monogram] and ear of barley seem to be the first posthumous emissions of that mint. It should be noted, however, that the last issue of Sardes, if it belongs to our Series XIII and was indeed in the hoard, was produced in the names of both Alexander IV and Philip III.

Gîldău (*IGCH* 774)

All ten Alexanders from this small pot hoard are illustrated in Bucur Mitrea's publication:

Macedonia

Fulmen (M. 6)
Cantharus (M. 10)
Trident (M. 3, 5)

Tarsus

Trident (M. 4; cf. Newell, *Tarsos*, 13)

Salamis

Spear-head (M. 7; cf. Newell, *NC* 1915, 5)
Rudder (M. 9; cf. Newell 11)

Miletus

Ear of barley, bipennis (T. 127a; M. 1)

Lampsacus

Foreparts of horses, [monogram] (M. 2)

Colophon

[monogram] above [monogram] (M. 8)

[65] See the commentary under Gîldău (p. 73).

The suggested burial date, c. 320 B.C., may be too early. Newell assigns Salamis coins with rudder symbol to the years 320-317 although he remarks (*NC* 1915, p. 314) that some may belong to the preceding period, 332-320, and Le Rider suggests (*Philippe*, p. 264) that the first rudder issues may have been struck just after the death of Alexander. The Colophonian stater, however, seems to postdate the death of Philip III.

Asia Minor 1964 (*IGCH* 1441)

Le Rider, *Philippe*, pp. 270-72

This important hoard, comprising staters of all seven Asia Minor mints except Colophon, is fully described and illustrated by Le Rider. The pertinent Alexander issues for Miletus and Sardes are as follows:

Miletus

ΗΑ (T. 7a; Le R. 34)

Sardes

Serpent (T. 14; Le R. 36)
Tripod (T. 31; Le R. 35)
Bucranium (T. 37a; Le R. 37)

For the most part the composition is chronologically consistent. The Macedonian Philips include the last issues of Pella IIIB and Amphipolis IIIA, both groups dated by Le Rider c. 323/2 -c. 315 B.C. The latest posthumous Philips and Alexanders from Asia Minor are issues struck during the reign of Philip III and hence no later than 317 B.C. Of the two Sidonian staters, the later bears the name of Philip III and is dated 318/7. Mørkholm's burial date of c. 315 in *IGCH* is fully confirmed by the hoard as a whole, but it is said also to have contained six Alexanders of Babylon, one of which is tentatively dated by Nancy Waggoner to c. 311-309 B.C.

Paeonia (*IGCH* 410)

Le Rider, *Philippe*, pp. 298-304

Staters of Lampsacus, Abydus, Magnesia, Miletus and Sardes were present in this large hoard of mixed gold and silver. Le Rider adds a few pieces, on information from Pierre Strauss, to the listings in the sales catalogues.[66]

[66] Sotheby, Apr. 16, 1969 and Parke Bernet, Dec. 9, 1969.

Miletus
Alexander: ΗΑ (PB. 144 but the illustration is too poor for die identification)
ΚΗ, bipennis (T. 175b; S. 271)

Sardes
Alexander: Griffin's head (T. 21a; PB. 149)
Tripod (T. 30; PB. 147)
Philip III: ΜΗ, torch (T. 148: PB. 156)
ΤΙ, rose (T. 230; S. 356)
Α, torch (T. 298: S. 359)

A burial date shortly after 316/5 B.C. is based on the Macedonian tetradrachms of Philip II and confirmed by the Asia Minor material which extends through the reign of Philip III.

Jasna Poljana (*IGCH* 777)

M. Lazarov, "A Hoard of Gold Staters of the Macedonian Kings Philip II and Alexander III," *Noumismatika* 3.1 (1971), pp. 20-22 (in Bulgarian)

Le Rider, *Philippe*, pp. 266-67.

Plate 33

In the original publication by Lazarov, 22 staters from the hoard are illustrated but by only one side of each coin. While assembling material for his study of Philip II, Georges Le Rider was able to obtain a full record of the 10 Philip staters for incorporation in his book. Through the kindness of Ivan Karayotov of the Burgas Museum and Jordanka Youroukova of the Sophia Museum, photographs of 12 Alexander staters were made available to me.

Eight of the Philips are from the mints of Pella and Amphipolis, the latest being Le Rider's 465b which is dated c. 323/2 -c. 315 B.C. The remaining two Philips come from Asia Minor: one from Abydus and the other from Teos. Both are from the time of Philip III.

The Alexanders illustrated here are from the following mints:

Amphipolis
11-12. Fulmen
13. Cantharus
14-15. Trident

Lampsacus
16. Foreparts of horses, ♁

Abydus

17. ΦΙΛΙΠΠΟΥ. Ϻ above serpent
18. Ϻ above pentagram and cornucopiae

Magnesia

19. Ram's head on obverse; ram's head on reverse

Sardes

20-21. Serpent (T. 11c, 12b)
22. Bucranium (T. 35a)

Citium

23. Ͱ

Alexandria

24. Rose, ΔΙ

Chronologically the two lots of staters are in complete accord. The Alexanders are lifetime or early posthumous issues, the latest dating from the reign of Philip III. Nothing in the hoard as we know it points to burial after c. 315 B.C.

Abusir (*IGCH* 1672)

Since there is no detailed record of the contents of this pot hoard of staters and tetradrachms of Philip II and Alexander III, the find is useless for chronological purposes. It contained at least one early stater of Miletus (T. 18a).

Larnaca (*IGCH* 1472)

Le Rider, *Philippe*, pp. 277-78

All seven of our Asia Minor mints are included in the listing prepared by Martin Price (*NC* 1969, pp. 4-8). Thirteen Alexanders of Miletus and Sardes can be identified:

Miletus

Ϻ (T. 18c, 21b; P. 48-9)
Ear of barley, bipennis (T. 126; P. 50)
Ʞ, bipennis (T. 170a; P. 51)

Sardes

Stag's head (T. 3b; P. 58)
Griffin's head (T. 20; P. 121)
ΤΙ, torch (T. 221a; P. 56)
ΤΙ, torch (T. 221e, 221c; P. 54-55)
ΤΙ, leaf (T. 224c; P. 57)

TI, bee (T. 225a; P. 52)
A, star (T. 359); P. 59)
⋈, star (T. 387a; P. 133)

Price and Le Rider agree on a burial c. 300 B.C. Most of the Asia Minor coinage was struck well before that date but there are some issues that belong to the last decade of the fourth century.

Thoricos (*IGCH* 134)

J. Bingen, "Le trésor monétaire Thorikos 1969," *Thorikos* 6 (1969), pp. 7-59

Three Alexander-type staters and one of Philip II were included in this large hoard of Athenian silver, which Bingen believes was buried in the first decade of the third century. Its two Asia Minor staters date from the time of Philip III.

Sardes
Philip III: TI (not KI) above bee (T. 225d; B. 2)

Colophon (not Magnesia)
Philip II: Tripod (B. 4)

No. Greece ante 1966 (*IGCH* 801)

Le Rider, *Philippe*, pp. 269-70 (no. 11) and 273-76 (no. 13)

Plate 37

Full details of the contents are given by Le Rider. Only eight staters are from Miletus and Sardes, all of the Alexander type.

Miletus
ΗΙ (T. 6b, 10)
Ear of barley, bipennis (T. 129)

Sardes
Serpent (T. 7b, 9a, 11b)
Bucranium (T. 33, 35b)

In the *IGCH* entry it was suggested that this hoard has survived in two sections: 100 staters seen and photographed by Pierre Strauss in 1969 and about 75 staters seen by an ANS correspondent in Greece in the late 1960s. Although admitting the possibility that the two lots belong together, Le Rider felt it unlikely since he had traced four of Strauss's staters to sales catalogues of 1959, thus establishing an interval of roughly 10 years between the appearance of the two bodies of material.

Actually Le Rider's discovery makes it even more probable that they are indeed one and the same hoard. The correspondent who provided the ANS with information had seen his 75 staters in the late 1960s but his letter of July 1969 states that according to his source "the hoard has been in the hands of its present owner for some ten years, individual pieces having been sold off from time to time." Since the hoard recorded by Strauss is said to have contained originally about 350 staters, it seems highly likely that the 75 coins seen in Greece by the ANS correspondent represent a second major portion of the find and should be associated with the 100 staters seen by Strauss.

Unfortunately only eight staters from this second lot, four of Philip II and four of Alexander, can be definitely identified. Seven are reproduced on Plate 37.

Tarsus
Alexander: 1-2. Θ on obverse; caduceus, Ε and Θ on reverse (same pair of dies and same obverse die as Newell, *Tarsos*, 52-O)

Babylon
Alexander: 3. [monogram], ΗΡ
4. Χ, [monogram]

Pella
Philip II: 5. Σ, trident (*Philippe* 588b)
6. Boeotian shield (*Philippe* 606d)

Magnesia
Philip II: 7. Bee, spear-head

Uncertain
Philip II: 8. Lyre

The first seven coins present no problems of chronology given a burial date toward the end of the fourth century for the Strauss lot. Newell dates the Tarsus Alexanders c. 324-319, while Nancy Waggoner assigns those of Babylon to the period 316-310 B.C. The Philips of Pella belong to the final years of Le Rider's Group IIIB, c. 315 or slightly earlier, and the Philip of Magnesia was issued during the joint reign of Philip III and Alexander IV.

It is the eighth coin which is of special interest. In style, it is clearly later than the other Philips and indeed finds its closest parallel in issues of the Maeander Valley Hoard published by Martin Price (*NC* 1969, pp. 9-10). One might even suggest that it shares a mint with one of the Maeander staters: Price 11 with AN below the horses (Plate 37, A). A stater in a recent Leu sale (May 5, 1977, 121 and Plate 37, B) is, as Silvia Hurter points out, from the same pair of dies as the Price specimen but the Leu coin has a small lyre in the lower right field.[67] Although the lyre in one case is a chelys and in the other a cithara, both types of lyre appear on the autonomous coinage of Mytilene and it is to that mint that one might tentatively assign the two Philip issues.

[67] The symbol, which is not visible on the BM coin, was probably added to the original die.

If we are dealing with a single hoard from northern Greece in which this lyre stater was included, then the burial date of the deposit should be lowered to about the time of the Maeander Valley interment. Price would place this in the early part of the third century since he finds the fourth-century Philips of Maeander Valley comparable in condition to similar issues of the Larnaca Hoard, buried c. 300 B.C. Any closer chronological definition must await a systematic analysis of the entire group of third-century Philips, which is beyond the scope of the present study. It is evident, however, that the phenomenon was not confined to the mints already identified: Magnesia, Mylasa, Mytilene and Rhodes.[68] In all probability Abydus, Ephesus and Teos or Phocaea also produced late posthumous Philips of roughly contemporary date:

Plate 37, C — Abydus with eagle and ⋈ (ANS, 8.46↑)
D — Ephesus with ΕΦ above bee (Kress 127, Oct. 23, 1963, 357, 8.50)[69]
E — Teos or Phocaea with head and neck of griffin (Hermitage, Anadol Hoard, 8.52)

Apparently these were brief and small emissions if one can judge by the fact that many of the staters are unique specimens. They must have been struck when the mints in question enjoyed a measure of autonomy but did not feel sufficiently secure to produce coinage in precious metals with their own autonomous types. It is possible that the striking took place soon after the death of Lysimachus in 281 B.C. and that of Seleucus I in the following year. Although Corupedium gave the Seleucids hegemony over Asia Minor, the period that followed was one of confusion and uncertainty. As Newell's survey shows, there is practically nothing in the way of Seleucid coinage from western Asia Minor until the latter part of the reign of Antiochus I.[70] During the preceding decade, 280-270, a number of Asia Minor mints, such as Parium, Chios and Lampsacus, were producing posthumous Alexander tetradrachms and drachms as civic issues.[71] One might suggest that at the same time other mints in the area were taking advantage of their quasi-independent status to put out a new series of the posthumous Philip staters which had played such an important role in the economy of the region during the fourth century.[72]

[68] See Price, p. 10, n. 1 for the addition of Rhodes. An example of the coinage is illustrated in the sale of the Ashburnham Collection (Sotheby May 6, 1895, 76).

[69] The date of the catalogue raises the possibility that this stater is also from the No. Greece Hoard.

[70] *WSM*, pp. 281-358, covering Caria, Ionia, Aeolis, Mysia and Thrace.

[71] H. Seyrig, "Parion au 3e siècle avant notre ére," *ANSCent.*, p. 614. See also R. Bauslaugh, "The Posthumous Alexander Coinage of Chios," *ANSMN* 24 (1979), pp. 1-12.

[72] The limited number of gold Philips from Miletus and Sardes gives no true indication of the extent of the coinage. There were substantial emissions at Lampsacus and Abydus, sizable ones at Magnesia, Colophon and Teos.

Malko Topolovo (*IGCH* 853)

Le Rider, *Philippe*, pp. 279-80

Miletus

[monogram] (T. 3a, 21b)
[monogram], bipennis (T. 174b, 176b)
[monogram], bipennis (T. 205?)

Sardes

Serpent (T. 11a)

The casts on file at the ANS are in very poor condition. Four Milesian Alexanders can be identified by dies; a fifth coin (T. 205) in Berlin is possibly from the hoard. An example of the early serpent emission of Sardes is present as are Philip II staters of Lampsacus and Colophon. Since this is a third-century hoard, interred c. 285-275 B.C., it is of no chronological importance for the present study.

Anadol (*IGCH* 866)

Le Rider, *Philippe*, 282-83

Miletus

Ear of barley, bipennis (T. 129; P. 238)
[monogram], bipennis (T. 176b; P. 239. T. 176c; P. 244)
Helmet crest, bipennis (T. 225; P. 436. T. 227)
[monogram], bipennis (T. 258b; P. 437)

Sardes

Serpent (T. 9a; P. 226)
TI, torch (T. 221e; P. 4)
A, torch with the name of Philip III (T. 298; P. 1)

The find also contained staters of Lampsacus, Abydus, Colophon and Magnesia. Some of the Hermitage entries in the present catalogues can be linked with Anadol on the basis of Pridik's illustrations but the record is obviously incomplete. The burial date of the hoard, c. 228-220 B.C. according to Seyrig, is too late for it to have any chronological significance in terms of the earlier material.

Mărășești (*IGCH* 958)

Gh. Poenaru Bordea, "Le trésor de Mărăşeşti," *Dacia* 18 (1974), pp. 103-25
Le Rider, *Philippe*, p. 284

Twenty-one Alexander staters of Lampsacus, Abydus and Miletus are published by Poenaru Bordea.

Miletus

ꞰΗ, bipennis (PB. 31-32 of which only 31 is illustrated and die identifications are uncertain)
Helmet crest, bipennis (T. 225; PB. 34)
Imitation? (T. 224; PB. 33)

Numerous posthumous Lysimachi from Byzantium and Euxine mints place the burial in the early first century B.C.

Four other hoards have Miletus-Sardes material which cannot be associated with specific catalogue entries.

Krivodol (*IGCH* 408) has two staters of Miletus (both with ear of barley and bipennis) and one of Sardes (bee above TI). A communication from T. Gerasimov lists three more coins: a Philip II stater of Teos (Σ and spear-head), a Macedonian Alexander (trident above Δ), and a Babylonian Alexander (ΛY). The seventh component of the small pot hoard is not described. Since the material from Asia Minor, Babylon and possibly Macedonia as well dates from the time of Philip III, the association of issues is chronologically consistent.

Ougri (*IGCH* 121) includes a Milesian stater of uncertain type in a mixed gold and silver deposit. A Philip II stater of Pella, two tetradrachms of Athens and four tetradrachms of Alexander were also acquired by the Athens Cabinet. The hoard record is almost certainly incomplete.

Aisaros River (*IGCH* 1955) with a number of Alexander staters which can be identified from von Duhn's list and among them Asia Minor issues: ꞰΗ and bipennis from Miletus and foreparts of horses and ⚲ from Lampsacus. The hoard is said to have been acquired by the Berlin Cabinet but Hans-Dietrich Schultz tells me that the Alexander and Philip material is not there and that he doubts it ever was. In any case, this is a late deposit, interred c. 290 according to Kraay.

Gravena (*IGCH* 148) is a large hoard of staters, partially recorded by E. T. Newell. The Asia Minor section includes the following issues:

Lampsacus — foreparts of horses and ⚲ (two examples), Ƨ and ⌂, forepart of Pegasus and AI.

Abydus — Ξ and horse's leg, Ⲙ or Ⲙ and ? (two examples), Ⲙ with pentagram and cornucopiae (two examples).

Magnesia — ram's head and ΗΡ, Ⲁ with seal and thyrsus, Ⲁ and ☉.

Teos — Π and Ψ, Ε and griffin.

Sardes — TI and leaf, Α and torch.

Miletus — ꞰΗ and bipennis, Ξ above bipennis, uncertain monogram above bipennis.

Burial c. 280 B.C. is likely in that numerous staters of Lysimachus and one of Seleucus I were mixed with the Alexander material. The hoard is too late to be of significance for the dating of the Asia Minor coins, but it is interesting to note the inclusion of two Milesian staters from the time of Demetrius Poliorcetes.

A number of additional hoards contain staters from Asia Minor mints but nothing from Sardes and Miletus. They will be discussed in connection with the publication of the Lampsacus and Abydus coinages.

SILVER HOARDS

About 50 deposits contain identifiable examples of the coinage of Miletus and Sardes from the last quarter of the fourth century and the first decade of the third. These hoards vary considerably in importance. Some are small accumulations which may or may not be complete records; in the latter case, if we had the entire hoard, the burial date might differ from the one suggested in the *IGCH*. Others, although probably intact finds, have only Alexandrine material and their burial dates often depend upon the tentative judgment of the editors of the *IGCH* with regard to the chronology of the mints represented. When we possess hoards with an admixture of Seleucid, Ptolemaic or Lysimachene coins, we are on safer ground for dating the burials, but such hoards are usually so late that they throw scant light on the chronology of the fourth-century strikings. Nevertheless all available evidence has been included in the section that follows.

Asia Minor 1964 (*IGCH* 1437)

Plates 34-37

For the early period of the coinage this is the most important drachm hoard on record.[73] It contained 88 coins from eight mints.

Amphipolis

1. *Rev.* to l., arrow. Hersh Coll., 4.28→

Lampsacus

2. *Rev.* to l., club. Hersh Coll., 4.30↑
3. *Obv.* of 2. *Rev.* as 2.

[73] The cooperation of the European dealer, who acquired the hoard, and of Charles Hersch, who supplied the photographic record, has made this publication possible. All pieces are illustrated with the exception of four die duplicates: nos. 27, 29, 61 and 70. About one-third of the hoard is now in the Hersh Collection and a few additional specimens were purchased by the ANS before the remaining material was dispersed.

4. *Rev.* to l., Artemis with torches; below, $\overset{\text{A}}{\text{O}}$. ANS, 4.30→
5. *Rev.* as 4 but with Δ below.
6. *Rev.* as 4.
7. *Rev.* as 4.
8. *Obv.* of 7. *Rev.* to l., ΑΓ . Hersh Coll, 4.30↑
9. *Obv.* and *rev.* of 8.
10. *Rev.* as 8.
11. *Rev.* as 8.

Abydus

12. *Rev.* to l., Hermes; below, Ξ . Hersh Coll., 4.25→
13. *Rev.* as 12 but with ΙΗ below. Hersh Coll., 4.29→
14. *Rev.* as 13.
15. *Obv.* of 14. *Rev.* as 13.
16. *Rev.* as 13.
17. *Rev.* as 13.
18. *Rev.* as 13.
19. *Rev.* as 13.
20. *Rev.* to l., forepart of Pegasus; below, $\overset{\text{I}}{\Omega}$.
21. *Rev.* as 20.
22. *Rev.* as 20. Hersh Coll., 4.33↑
23. *Rev.* as 20.
24. *Rev.* as 20.
25. *Rev.* as 20.
26. *Obv.* and *rev.* of 25.
27. *Obv.* and *rev.* of 25.
28. *Rev.* as 20.
29. *Obv.* and *rev.* of 28.
30. *Rev.* as 20.
31. *Obv.* and *rev.* of 30.
32. *Rev.* as 20.
33. *Obv.* and probably *rev.* of 32.
34. *Obv.* of 32. *Rev.* to l., $\overset{\text{I}}{\Omega}$ above forepart of Pegasus.
35. *Rev.* as 34.
36. *Obv.* and *rev.* of 35.
37. *Rev.* as 34. Hersh Coll., 4.26↑
38. *Obv.* and *rev.* of 37.
39. *Rev.* as 34.
40. *Obv.* of 39. *Rev.* to l., palm tree. Hersh Coll., 4.21↑
41. *Obv.* of 39. *Rev.* to l., palm tree; below, ΗΜ. Hersh Coll., 4.34↑
42. *Obv.* of 39. *Rev.* to l., palm tree above ΗΜ. Hersh Coll., 4.31→
43. *Obv.* of 39. *Rev.* to l., fish; below, ΔΥ . Hersh Coll., 4.32→

Sardes

44. *Rev.* to l., griffin's head (T. 25). Hersh Coll., 4.37↑
45. *Rev.* to l., bucranium (T. 39). Hersh Coll., 4.32↑
46. *Rev.* to l., 丰; below, rose (T. 58d). Hersh Coll., 4.26↑
47. *Rev.* below, rose (T. 83c). ANS, 4.28↑
48. *Rev.* as 47 (T. 84c). Hersh Coll., 4.31↑
49. *Rev.* as 47 (T. 94). Hersh Coll., 4.30↑
50. *Rev.* to l., Mithras head (T. 98). Hersh Coll., 4.30↑
51. *Rev.* to l., NK; below, torch (T. 125). Hersh Coll., 4.30↑
52. *Rev.* to l., 丰 above torch (T. 183b). Hersh Coll., 4.34↑
53. *Rev.* to l., 丰; below, torch (T. 192b). Hersh Coll., 4.27↑

Magnesia

54. *Rev.* to l., [monogram] ; below, ram's head facing. Hersh Coll., 4.28↓
55. *Rev.* to l., bee; below, ram's head facing; to r., spear-head. Hersh Coll., 4.28↑
56. *Obv.* of 55. *Rev.* as 55 but ram's head side view.
57. *Rev.* as 56.
58. *Rev.* as 56.
59. *Obv.* and *rev.* of 58.
60. *Obv.* and *rev.* of 58.
61. *Obv.* and *rev.* of 58.
62. *Obv.* and *rev.* of 58.
63. *Rev.* of 58.
64. *Obv.* and *rev.* of 63. Hersh Coll., 4.30↑
65. *Obv.* of 58. *Rev.* below, ram's head side view. Hersh Coll., 4.35↓
66. *Obv.* and *rev.* of 65. ANS, 4.31↓
67. *Rev.* of 65.[74] ANS, 4.31↑
68. *Rev.* to l., bucranium
69. *Obv.* and *rev.* of 68.
70. *Obv.* and *rev.* of 68. Hersh Coll., 4.34↑
71. *Obv.* and *rev.* of 68.
72. *Obv.* and *rev.* of 68. ANS, 4.36↑
73. *Rev.* to l., bucranium; to r., spear-head. Hersh Coll, 4.13↑
74. *Rev.* below, bee; to r., spear-head. ANS, 4.29↑
75. *Obv.* of 74. *Rev.* as 74. Hersh Coll., 4.26↑

Colophon

76. *Rev.* below, barleycorn; to r., spear-head.

Miletus

77. *Rev.* to l., ⋈ (T. 70). Hersh Coll., 4.30↑
78. *Rev.* as 77 (T. 84a).
79. *Rev.* as 77 (T. 86b).

[74] The obverse is very close to nos. 63-64 but not, I think, identical.

80. *Rev.* as 77 (T. 91a).
81. *Rev.* as 77 (T. 94b).
82. *Rev.* as 77 (T. 103a).
83. *Rev.* as 77 (T. 108). Hersh Coll., 4.31↑
84. *Rev.* as 77 (T. 110a).
85. *Obv.* of 84. *Rev.* as 77 (T. 110b).
86. *Rev.* as 77 (T. 116a). Hersh Coll., 4.29↑
87. *Rev.* to l., ear of barley (T. 139a).

Ake

88. *Rev.* to l., Phoenician letters and numerals (year 22).

The crucial coin is, of course, the dated drachm of Ake. Year 22 is the equivalent of 324 B.C.[75] and the excellent condition of the piece attests limited circulation. Even allowing an interval for it to reach Asia Minor and be incorporated into the body of hoard material, the burial of the deposit must be close to the time of Alexander's death. That it took place a few years later is established by several issues of the Asia Minor mints.

Since all coins bear the Alexander legend, one might assume that they antedate the joint reign of Philip III and the young Alexander but this is not the case. Coins inscribed with the name of Philip are known for the last Magnesian issue, that with bee and spear-head (nos. 74-75); they are also known for the final issue at Sardes (nos. 52-53). In fact the emission immediately preceding, with [monogram] but not represented in the hoard, was struck in the names of both Philip and Alexander. Furthermore posthumous staters of Philip II type are associated with the last issue at Lampsacus (nos. 8-11) and the last two at Abydus (nos. 40-43). If, as Le Rider postulates in his superb study of the coinage of Philip II,[76] there was a period between 328 and 323 when gold Philips ceased to be struck at Pella and Amphipolis and if, as seems likely, the situation was similar in Asia Minor, then the latest hoard coins of Lampsacus and Abydus belong to the early years of the joint reign.[77] All in all the evidence for a burial date c. 321 B.C., as given in the *IGCH*, is very strong.

Practically without exception the coins of the hoard are in very good to mint state of preservation.[78] Indeed the amount of die duplication, particularly in the case of Abydus and Magnesia, suggests that many of the drachms had come from the mint only a short time before burial. The last three issues of Abydus are represented by 24 coins, produced from 12 obverse and 16 reverse dies. The entire sequence at Magnesia (22

[75] E. T. Newell, *Sidon and Ake*, p. 43 for tetradrachms; no drachms are recorded for this date.

[76] *Philippe*, pp. 435-37.

[77] Although the first appearance of Philip II staters at several Asia Minor mints was dated c. 324 in the publication of the Bab Hoard (*IGCH* 1534), the chronology there given was to some extent tentative. There is no apparent obstacle to a slightly later date for the issues involved.

[78] This is true of even the earliest examples. These would include the Amphipolis drachm of c. 326 (see p. 88 under Sinan Pascha for the date), and the initial issues of Lampsacus, Sardes and Magnesia which may be a few years earlier.

coins) is from 9 obverse and 10 reverse dies: 10 coins of the bee-ram's head-spear striking from 4 obverses and 4 reverses while all 5 coins with bucranium alone are from a single pair of dies. Lampsacus has some duplication, Miletus one example and Sardes none. Linkage between issues within the same mint adds nothing to the existing record.

The representation of mints is decidedly unbalanced. There is nothing from Teos, which is not surprising since it was a minor mint and may have begun its Alexander coinage only shortly before the hoard was buried. The presence of only one Colophonian drachm is, however, puzzling for the barleycorn issue of that mint was a very large one and certainly in production well before 321 B.C. Neighboring Magnesia on the other hand supplied the second largest number of hoard coins. At this period the output of Lampsacus and Abydus was roughly comparable, yet Lampsacus's contribution to the hoard was only a third that of Abydus. One wonders if the distribution of small change to various parts of Asia Minor followed a certain pattern, with the region in which our hoard was buried drawing largely from a single Hellespontine and a single Ionian workshop. To define that region more closely would be impossible, although, considering the hoard's burial date, one might suggest that it lay in the path of the military operations of Craterus and Eumenes.[79]

Thessaly 1966

Coin Hoards 2, p. 20, 51-52

Two drachms of Miletus ([monogram]) and one of Magnesia (thyrsus) were in the hoard; one Milesian piece is illustrated in the publication (T. 54b). Price places the burial c. 323-320 B.C. The later date is more likely in view of the absence of the thyrsus issue from the Asia Minor 1964 Hoard (see above) which contained so much Magnesian material.

Demanhur (*IGCH* 1664)

Miletus

2 [monogram] (T. 24b, 27b)
4 Ear of barley (T. 134a, 137a, 137e, 138)
1 [monogram] (T. 158c)
2 [monogram] - [monogram] (T. 160, 160)
5 [monogram] (T. 181d, 182a, 183b, 183b, 183e)

Sardes

1 Bucranium (T. 38)
1 Mithras head - trisceles (T. 46)
1 [monogram] (T. 53)

[79] Diodorus 18.29-31. The battle which cost Craterus his life took place in the Hellespont area and is dated 321/0 by the Parian Marble.

The burial date of 318 B.C. is especially significant for the coinage of Miletus; its last issue must have been struck prior to that year and is accordingly dated c. 319. There is very little tetradrachm coinage from Sardes during this early period but its TI issue is a fairly large one, probably also produced c. 319 although not present in Demanhur. The absence may be accounted for by the greater distance between Sardes and Egypt. Numerous drachms with TI were included in the Sinan Pascha Hoard, buried c. 317/6 at a place much closer to Sardes than Demanhur.

Sinan Pascha (*IGCH* 1395)

Plate 38

The New York portion of this drachm hoard was acquired by E. T. Newell over a period of years. According to his records, a number of small lots were obtained from a London dealer in 1919 and later. Newell himself purchased over 400 pieces from several Athenian dealers in 1920-21, and Sydney P. Noe found additional specimens in Athens a few years afterwards. Other lots came between 1924 and 1927 from a dealer in the United States.

Although Newell had no illusions about having secured the entire hoard, he was confident that these various lots derived from the same find despite the diverse geographical and chronological circumstances of acquisition. As supporting evidence, he cited the consistently fine condition of the coins and a similarity of patination: "very thin patches of purple oxide with a light brownish discoloration of the remaining portions of the surfaces."[80]

No precise information on the findspot was available from the dealers who provided Newell's specimens. The Athenian sections were said to have been brought from Asiatic Turkey. Other lots were described as "from near Chesmé" and "from near Afyon-Karahissar." The Istanbul Cabinet, which obtained 30 drachms from the hoard, recorded them as coming from Sinan Pascha, which is near Afyon-Karahissar. Whatever the exact location, it seems highly likely that the discovery was made in the general vicinity of Phrygian Prymnessus.[81]

Since the hoard supplies much of the tangible and chronological evidence for the output of Alexander's drachm mints between 330 and 316 B.C., it merits detailed analysis. Representation of mints in New York is as follows:[82]

[80] Subsequent cleaning has removed this evidence but there is no reason to question Newell's observations made at the time the coins reached him.

[81] A degree of confirmation is provided by the relative representation of mints. Sardes, the site closest to Sinan Pascha, has the largest number of coins, followed by the Ionian mints of Colophon and Magnesia, with Miletus also well represented. On the other hand the Hellespontine centers of Lampsacus and Abydus, with extensive drachm coinages at this early period, are present in comparatively short supply.

[82] Catalogue numbers for Sardes and Miletus are not given because of the large amount of coinage involved, but a breakdown by issues is provided on the Hoard Chart (p. 98). Similar charts will be included in publications of the other major mints.

Miletus	73
Sardes	177
Colophon	170
Magnesia	74
Teos	15
Lampsacus	61
Abydus	48
Miscellaneous	22
	640[83]

The 22 miscellaneous drachms are reproduced on Plate 38.[84]

Amphipolis

1. *Rev.* to l., arrow. 4.24↓
2. *Obv.* and *rev.* of 1. 4.23↓
3. *Rev.* to l., ᒥ. 4.29↓

Side[85]

4. *Rev.* below, A. 4.01↑
5. *Rev.* as 4. 4.08↑
6. *Obv.* of 5. *Rev.* as 4. 4.38↑
7. *Obv.* and *rev.* of 6. 4.21↑
8. *Rev.* to l., pomegranate (?); below, ΠΥ. 4.15↑
9. *Rev.* ΦΙΛΙΓΓΟΥ; to l., pomegranate; below, ΠΥ. 4.27↑
10. *Rev.* ΦΙΛΙΓΓΟΥ; to l., pomegranate; below, Λ. 4.30↑
11. *Rev.* of 10. 4.26↑

Aradus

12. *Rev.* ΒΑΣΙΛΕΩΣ ΑΛΕΞΑΝΔΡΟΥ; to l., Σ; below, Α. 4.15↑
13. *Rev.* as 12. 4.29↓
14. *Rev.* probably as 12. 4.31→
15. *Rev.* ΒΑΣΙΛΕΩΣ ΑΛΕΞΑΝΔΡΟΥ; to l., Ι ; below, Α. 4.24→

[83] The total in *IGCH* is 682: New York 652 and Istanbul 30. In large measure the discrepancy is accounted for by the exclusion of seven coins from the helmet crest issue of Miletus. As noted in the commentary on Series IX (p. 61) this emission is die-linked to one which forms part of the coinage of Demetrius Poliorcetes at Miletus in the years after Ipsus. It must date c. 300 B.C. and its coins cannot belong to the Sinan Pascha Hoard. One of the pieces, moreover, shows distinct signs of wear.

The presence of a few intrusions in a very large hoard, assembled in various lots at various times, is scarcely surprising. It does, of course, open the possibility of other intrusive material. One can only judge the case of any additional "suspect" entries on the basis of the evidence as a whole.

[84] No attempt has been made to illustrate the hoard in its entirety. Due to their excellent condition, the Sinan coins from the major mints are well represented on the regular plates.

[85] For the attribution of nos. 4-7, see M. Thompson, "The Cavalla Hoard," *ANSMN* 26 (1981), pp. 44-48.

Babylon

16. *Rev.* to l., M; below, [monogram]. 4.25↗
17. *Rev.* as 16. 4.26→
18. *Rev.* as 16. 4.23←
19. *Rev.* ΒΑΣΙΛΕΩΣ ΑΛΕΞΑΝΔΡΟΥ; to l., M; below, ΛΥ. 4.27←

Uncertain

20. *Obv.* below neck, E. *Rev.* below, uncertain symbol or monogram. 4.24↑
21. *Rev.* to l., lion's head; to r., ear of grain. 4.32↓
22. *Rev.* ΦΙΛΙΠΠΟΥ; to l., star; below, ΦΙΛ. 4.27↑

For the most part there is nothing unusual about the presence of these stray pieces. A few drachms of Amphipolis, Side, Aradus and Babylon are also found in the later Cavalla and Armenak Hoards, in which the bulk of the drachm material derives from the same mints as those of Sinan Pascha.

The four coins of Side with pomegranate symbol are from the time of Philip III; those with A (nos. 4-7) are, I believe, roughly contemporary issues from the same workshop. Newell dates Aradus tetradrachms with Σ and I in the left field between 327 and 319 B.C.,[86] while the Babylonian drachms are to be associated with tetradrachms of c. 326 (nos. 16-18) and 323-320 (no. 19). The M-ΛΥ of the last entry is found on coins struck in the names of both Alexander and Philip III.[87]

The material from Amphipolis is of greater interest. That mint produced very little in the way of drachm coinage of the standard Alexander type, but examples of the arrow issue are known. Just where they belong in the overall sequence is somewhat uncertain since there are no tetradrachms with the same symbol. In style nos. 1-2 seem closest to the Demanhur tetradrachms of Newell's Group F, dated c. 326 B.C.,[88] and the arrow would be a logical abbreviation for the bow and quiver which appear on some of the larger coins.

No. 3 is exceedingly rare. Its obverse style is that of Amphipolis and its reverse marking, Γ in the left field,[89] links it with a large series of tetradrachms from that mint, some with the types of Philip II and some with those of Alexander. These tetradrachms, absent from Demanhur, are the immediate successors of coins with Γ alone, which comprise the final strikings of the Demanhur deposit.[90] The new drachm then would date the burial of Sinan Pascha slightly later than that of Demanhur.

[86] *Demanhur*, pp. 51-52.

[87] *Demanhur*, pp. 60, 63.

[88] *Demanhur*, p. 29; examples of the issues are illustrated on plate 8 of *Reattribution*. Compare nos. 1-4 for the obverse style.

[89] Although the dot within the Γ does not reproduce clearly, it is very definitely present on the coin.

[90] Newell (*Demanhur*, p. 32) places an issue with [monogram] -Λ at the very end but I would agree with Le Rider (*Philippe*, p. 397, n. 5) that it more likely comes before rather than after the Γ issues.

Concerning the three uncertain pieces there is little to be said. On the evidence of style, no. 20 should be a lifetime or very early posthumous striking but it cannot be associated with a known mint and the marking below the stool is illegible. No. 21 may be intrusive. Although it was with the other hoard coins, its ticket says that it was obtained from an American dealer in 1931 and the late date makes its connection with the hoard somewhat suspect. The last coin, no. 22, belongs to the time of Philip III but its mint has not been identified.

In some miscellaneous notes on Sinan Pascha, Newell writes "what the great Demanhur Hoard accomplished for the correct understanding of the probable sequence of the early tetradrachms of Alexander and Philip III, the present hoard does for the corresponding drachms." And a little later he comments "the issues run down to c. 317/6, the date of burial." No reasons are given but the picture is clear, particularly with respect to Sardes.[91] In the Egyptian deposit of 318 B.C., there is not a single example of the sizable issue of TI tetradrachms or of the smaller issue with A. The relevant drachms, however, are present in Sinan Pascha: 65 with TI and 7 with A. The evidence from Sardes, combined with that from Amphipolis, places the burial of Sinan Pascha about the time of the assassination of Philip III.

Abu Hommos (*IGCH* 1667)

Miletus

1 [monogram] (T. 27a)
2 [monogram] - [monogram] (T. 162a, 165a)
5 [monogram] (T. 181a, 181a, 181d, 181e, 181f)

Sardes

2 TI (T. 231, 232b)
1 A with the name of Philip (T. 307)

The latest tetradrachm is the issue of Philip III, struck some years before Newell's burial date of 311/0 B.C.

Kuft (*IGCH* 1670)

D. Nash, "The Kuft Hoard of Alexander III Tetradrachms," *NC* 1974, pp. 14-30.

The following 17 tetradrachms are recorded by Nash as part of the Kuft Hoard; only 11 can be associated with catalogue entries:

Miletus

2 [monogram] (1 = T. 158f)
3 [monogram] - [monogram]
6 [monogram] (4 = T. 181d, 182b, 182c, 183c)

[91] For Miletus the only tetradrachm issue of this early period not represented in Demanhur is that with [monogram] (Series VIII, p. 59), known from a single specimen. Its absence from the hoard may be sheer chance.

Sardes

- 2 TI-leaf (T. 234b, 235a)
- 4 TI-torch (T. 237a, 238b, 239b, 239g)

Coins of Sidon (312/1) and Ake (311/0) provide the evidence for interment c. 310-305, the date of both Newell and Jenkins. Nash prefers the later date, c. 305. Since the Asia Minor material above was minted before the death of Philip III, there is no chronological significance in its inclusion in the hoard.[92]

Aksaray (*IGCH* 1400)

Two coins of Sardes are among the 19 tetradrachms of this small pot hoard:

Star above F-A (T. 372b; P. 5)
[monogram]-[monogram] (T. 393; P. 6)[93]

The latest dated piece is an issue of Seleucus I (*ESM* 4) of 305/4 according to Newell. In the original publication Pfeiler suggests a burial between 304 and 300 B.C., perhaps to be associated with military operations of Seleucus against Antigonus. This accords well with the probable chronology of the late third-century tetradrachms of Sardes.

In the *IGCH* the burial date of 281 B.C. represents a later revision by Pfeiler in his publication of the Manissa Hoard (*IGCH* 1293). There he cites Nancy Waggoner's rearrangement of the emissions of Seleucus at Seleucia,[94] which would date the Aksaray coin c. 292-280 B.C. With the exception of this one tetradrachm, however, the hoard closes c. 300 or a few years earlier and from the illustrations the Seleucid striking seems to be in no fresher condition than those of Sardes which must predate the issues of Lysimachus at that mint. Is the single Syrian coin perhaps intrusive?

Asia Minor 1961 (*IGCH* 1444)

The bulk of the hoard (173 coins) passed through the hands of a European dealer who sent photographs to Charles Hersh; the cooperation of the latter makes it possible to present a detailed record here. An additional 27 drachms, undoubtedly from the same deposit, were secured by an American dealer and casts were taken at the ANS. All coins are Alexander-type drachms with the exception of three hemidrachms of Cius, discussed by Georges Le Rider[95] and dated c. 330-320 B.C. or possibly even earlier.

[92] Actually the composition of the hoard is not certain. See O. Zervos, "The Delta Hoard of Ptolemaic Alexanders, 1896." *ANSMN* 21 (1976), pp. 51-52 and "Newell's Manuscript of the Kuft Hoard," *ANSMN* 25 (1980), pp. 17-29.

[93] Listed by Pfeiler as Miletus?

[94] "The Early Alexander Coinage at Seleucia on the Tigris," *ANSMN* 15 (1969), pp. 21-30, esp. 27.

[95] *Deux trésors de monnaies grecques de la Propontide* (Paris, 1963), p. 31.

Twelve coins of Sardes and three of Miletus can be identified by catalogue numbers in the listing below. The hoard as a whole was composed as follows:

Lampsacus	39
Abydus	88
Colophon	44
Magnesia	9
Teos	1
Sardes	12 (T. 110a, 149b, 183a, 243, 278b, 334a, 337, 345a, 352a-b, 355b-c)
Miletus	3 (T. 51, 82c, 115)
Side	1 (A below stool)[96]
Cius	3 (autonomous)

A burial date c. 300 B.C. is established by the presence of one drachm of Lysimachus from Abydus with forepart of lion and Alexander legend and by the large number of drachms from Lampsacus of an issue die-linked to the first coinage of Lysimachus at that mint. Given the presence of the Cius hemidrachms and the heavy proportion of drachms from the two Hellespont centers, it seems reasonably certain that burial took place somewhere in northwestern Asia Minor.

Phacous (*IGCH* 1678)

In addition to one early tetradrachm of Lampsacus (Artemis-♀) the pertinent Asia Minor material includes:

Miletus

1 [monogram]
3 [monogram] - [monogram]
6 KH

Sardes

2 TI-torch
1 ꟻ-A
2 [monogram] above star (T. 382a; J. pl. 3, 4)

The latest dated tetradrachms in Jar 1, which held the Attic weight coins, are from Ake (307/6) and Sidon (306/5). Jenkins thought the hoarder put aside the heavier coins from outside Egypt until c. 305 B.C. In discussing the Kuft Hoard (see above, p. 89), Nash argued that the date should be lowered to c. 300 or even later and this is to some extent confirmed by the Sardes material. All 10 coins of Miletus and the TI pieces of Sardes belong to the time of Philip III but the last issue at Sardes was probably struck after 305 or so close to that date that the coins could scarcely have reached Egypt by 305.

[96] For the attribution see the publication of the Cavalla Hoard (above, n. 85).

Aleppo (*IGCH* 1516)

Newell's hoard notebook records a considerable portion of this very large deposit of tetradrachms and drachms. Although only one catalogue entry can be identified as coming from Aleppo,[97] the hoard is significant for the chronology and sequence of the late tetradrachms of Sardes.

Miletus

Drachms: 2 Ⱨ [monogram]	Tetradrachms: 1 Ear of barley
	1 ꟼ [monogram] (T. 158c)
	1 Ⱨ [monogram]

Sardes

Drachms: 2 ꟽ [monogram]	Tetradrachms: 1 Bucranium
2 TI	7 TI
1 A	8 A-star
	4 Γ-A-star
	4 ₣-A [monogram]
	11 ₼-star [monogram]

All 27 late tetradrachms of Sardes are described by Newell as in fine to mint state, the best being the 11 pieces with ₼-star [monogram].

Of the coins that Newell records, the latest dated specimens are from Sidon (308/7) and Ake (305); presumably they are the basis for his burial date of c. 305 B.C. There are, however, three drachms which indicate that this date is somewhat early: two from an issue die-linked to the first coinage of Lysimachus at Lampsacus and another, from Abydus, which was struck shortly before Lysimachus began using that mint. Furthermore, some at least of the late material from Sardes was in all probability issued after 305. The Aleppo Hoard seems to be a deposit of c. 300 or even slightly later. Its "fine to mint" Sardes tetradrachms would belong to the preceding decade and of the four issues represented, that with ₼-star [monogram] would be the latest.

Mosul 1862 (*IGCH* 1756)

There is a tetradrachm of Abydus, one of Miletus and two of Sardes.

Miletus: Ⱨ [monogram]

Sardes: Γ-A above star
₼-star [monogram]

The latest dated coin is from Sidon (306/5). A burial c. 300 is likely; Newell also felt it was "after 305."

[97] Almost certainly other entries from the Vienna Cabinet belong to Aleppo although not so indicated on the casts Newell had assembled.

Mesopotamia 1954 (*IGCH* 1751)

In the *IGCH* the burial date of c. 315 B.C. is given on Seyrig's authority but this must be a mistake.[98] The only coin from our mints is a tetradrachm of Sardes with star above Ϙ to left, Α below the stool, and an amphora to the right. This is described as "assez bien." There is also a tetradrachm of Ake which Seyrig carefully identifies as Newell 44 (obv. die 38) and thus a striking of c. 309/8 B.C. It is also "assez bien" as is another tetradrachm with forepart of a lion to left and an uncertain monogram below the stool. Although this is unidentifiable by mint, it is surely an issue of Lysimachus. The hoard cannot have been buried prior to 300 B.C. and it may well be somewhat later.

Asia Minor 1965 (*IGCH* 1443)

Three tetradrachms of Sardes represent our Asia Minor mints:

ΤΙ-torch
Α-star
Ꞩ- ⱳ

The latest dated coin is one of Ake from 313 B.C. but the Sardes issues go beyond that date, the last probably struck only shortly before Lysimachus gained control of the city. Burial c. 300 is more likely than c. 310.

Thessalonica (*IGCH* 444)

From Newell's partial record, the hoard contained:

Miletus: 1 Ӿ-bipennis

Sardes: 1 ΤΙ-leaf
2 Α-star
1 ⱳ -star

The Milesian coin, the latest, belongs to the time of Demetrius Poliorcetes, c. 300-295 B.C.

Megara (*IGCH* 137)

Newell's hoard book lists drachm varieties for five of our Asia Minor mints; nothing is recorded for Miletus or Teos.

Sardes: 1 Ѣ-rose
1 ΙΟΡ-torch
1 ΝΚ-bee

[98] Seyrig supplied the ANS with a list of the hoard pieces but without indication of any burial date.

1 ⍎-horse's leg (Philip III)
1 A-rose (Philip III)
2 ⋈-Ⓚ (1 = T. 403c)
1 ⋈-Ⓜ (T. 405b)

There are Alexander-type issues of Lysimachus from other mints but nothing with his name. Price's burial date, c. 295 B.C., may be slightly late.

Karaman (*IGCH* 1398)

A tetradrachm of Miletus with ⌶-bipennis (T. 249c; P. 5) is the latest coin in the hoard. Its association with the coinage of Demetrius Poliorcetes after Ipsus would lower Pfeiler's burial date to c. 295-290.

Paphos district (*IGCH* 1469)

As in the case of the hoard immediately preceding, the latest piece is a Milesian tetradrachm with ⌶-bipennis. Burial may have been connected with Ptolemy's seizure of Cyprus in 294 B.C. In any event the *IGCH* date of c. 310 is too early.

Asia Minor ante 1951 (*IGCH* 1445)

A drachm of Miletus with ⊛ -bipennis is securely identifiable as the last issue of Demetrius Poliorcetes at that mint. Like the two preceding entries, the hoard was probably buried c. 295-290 B.C.

Asia Minor 1970

M. Kampmann, "Un trésor d'Alexandres," *RN* 1972, pp. 151-68
Coin Hoards 1, p. 19, 55

This large hoard of tetradrachms was interred c. 282 B.C. on the evidence of its 12 Seleucid pieces. Eight coins of Miletus and nine of Sardes were in the deposit.[99]

Miletus
1 Ear of barley (T. 134b; K. 40)
6 ⌶-bipennis (T. 245, 247a, 248a, 249a, d and e = K. 44, 45, 46, 43, 42, 41)
1 ⋈-lion (K. 47)

Sardes
1 TI-torch (T. 236b; K. 32)
1 Γ-A-star (T. 369c; K. 38)
5 ⍏-star (T. 380d and e, 381c and e, 386f = K. 35, 36, 34, 33, 37)
2 ⋈ (T. 391f, 397a; K. 31, 39)

[99] I am grateful to M. Kampmann for photographs of coins not illustrated in *RN*, which have made die comparisons possible.

With the exception of the TI striking, from the time of Philip III, the Sardes material belongs to the last decade of the fourth century. The Milesian coins, again with the exception of the first entry, are even later: the six with monogram and bipennis from the years between 300 and 294 when Demetrius Poliorcetes used the mint and the last coin a civic issue to be dated after 294. It may in fact be one of the latest of the hoard coins.

In his publication, Kampmann points out that the absence of tetradrachms of Lysimachus is strange in a deposit from Asia Minor buried close to the time of his death. The hoard, however, is predominantly composed of eastern material. That it had no tetradrachms of Lampsacus, Abydus, Colophon, Magnesia and Teos is not surprising for those drachm mints struck little or no silver in large denomination after Alexander's death. What is surprising is the comparative scarcity of Macedonian material: only 24 tetradrachms from Amphipolis and 6 from Pella. Of the overall total of some 300 coins, 165 are of Babylon and most of the others come from mints in southern Anatolia, Cyprus, Syria, Phoenicia and further east. The impression is that of a Levantine hoard. If the discovery was made in Asia Minor, it must have been somewhere in the extreme south where Lysimachus seems never to have exercised firm control.[100] There is also a strong possibility that Asia Minor was merely a way station for a hoard unearthed in the Levant.

The following hoards, some of which have been fully published elsewhere, require no special comment. In general they contain only a small amount of Miletus-Sardes material, often identifiable by issue alone, and their burial dates are too late to be relevant for the chronology of the Asia Minor coinage.

"Tripolitsa" (*IGCH* 84). Newell's burial date is c. 315 B.C. The one tetradrachm of Miletus (T. 137b) was struck before 320.

Egypt 1894 (*IGCH* 1669). One tetradrachm of Lampsacus and one of Sardes (TI-torch) are earlier than Jenkins's burial date of c. 310 B.C.

Kannaviou (*IGCH* 1468). Martin Price has kindly provided specific information on the contents of this mixed hoard of tetradrachms and drachms, which Otto Mørkholm dates c. 310 B.C. *Miletus*: [monogram]. *Sardes*: [monogram]-rose with name of Philip III, [monogram]-torch, TI-bee, TI-? with name of Philip, A-bee. All Sardes issues belong to the time of Philip III; the Milesian coin is earlier.

Drama (*IGCH* 414). The two relevant drachms—Miletus with [monogram] and Sardes with rose below the stool—were in circulation well before Newell's burial date of 310-305.

Kato Paphos (*IGCH* 1471). Three drachms of Miletus and Sardes from the time of Philip III in a hoard buried c. 305.

Miletus: 1 with [monogram].

Sardes: 2 with A-torch (one in the name of Philip).

[100] At least it is noteworthy that he used no mints in that area; Magnesia was the southernmost source of his Asia Minor coinage.

Aghios Ioannis (*IGCH* 1470). One tetradrachm of Sardes (TI-torch) was struck during the reign of Philip III; another with star left may belong to the A-star issue of the same mint. If so, it is roughly contemporary with the dated coin of Sidon (307/6) which places burial c. 305 or a little later.

Aphrodisias (*IGCH* 1283). Published by K. Erim and D. MacDonald, "A Hoard of Alexander Drachms from Aphrodisias," *NC* 1974, pp. 174-76. The two relevant coins are not illustrated: *Miletus* with 𐅃; Sardes with 𐅃-rose. Both are considerably earlier than the suggested burial date of 305 or later.

Siphnos (*IGCH* 91). The hoard, published by Newell, is loosely dated c. 320-300. It had one drachm of the first Milesian issue with 𐅃 (T. 102; N. 30).

Izmit (*IGCH* 1365). Published by Le Rider and also dated 320-300. A drachm of Sardes with TI-bird from the time of Philip III (T. 259a; Le R. 433).

Mosul 1949 (*IGCH* 1758). This small hoard of drachms and hemidrachms, interred c. 310-300, contained single specimens of Colophon, Miletus (𐅃) and Sardes (A-torch).

Myriophyton (*IGCH* 432). One Sardes tetradrachm with ⩚-star was included along with numerous examples of the Λ-torch coinage of Cassander. Burial c. 300 or a little later is probable.

Ankara (*IGCH* 1399). The hoard, buried c. 290-285, is said to have contained two tetradrachms of Sardes. One with ⩚-star is at the ANS (T. 381d).

Kiouleler (*IGCH* 144). Newell's partial record of the tetradrachms includes:

Miletus: 1 ⊛-⊛ ; 2 ⊠-bipennis

Sardes: 1 A-star-leaf, 1 F-A-amphora, 1 ⩚-star, 1 ⊠-star.

The latest coins are the two with bipennis from Miletus, of the time of Demetrius Poliorcetes and therefore antedating by a decade or more the suggested burial date of 285-275 B.C.

Burial dates for the following hoards range from 280-200 B.C.

Epidaurus (*IGCH* 158). A tetradrachm of Miletus with ⊠-bipennis (T. 251).

Asia Minor c. 1967 (*IGCH* 1446).

Miletus: 1 𐅃-fulmen, 1 K̵H, 2 M

Sardes: 1 NK-torch, 1 𐅃-torch in the name of Philip, 1 A-torch

The autonomous issue of Miletus with M must come after 294 but is probably not much later.

Mersin (*IGCH* 1424). Two tetradrachms of Miletus with ⊠-bipennis (T. 247f, 252c) and one of Sardes with ⩚-star (T. 383d).

Pontoleibade-Kilkis (*IGCH* 445). Two identifiable tetradrachms of Sardes: one with F-A amphora (T. 379c) and one with ⊠ (T. 394e).

Manissa (*IGCH* 1293). One tetradrachm of Miletus with ear of barley (T. 137c; P. 7).

Cavalla (*IGCH* 450). For the publication of this ANS hoard, see M. Thompson, "A Hoard from Cavalla," *ANSMN* 26 (1981), pp. 33-49. A breakdown by issues for its 20 drachms of Miletus and 35 of Sardes is given on the Hoard Chart (p. 98).

Armenak (*IGCH* 1423). Another ANS hoard which is now being prepared for publication. Its 28 drachms of Miletus and 56 of Sardes are recorded by issues on the Hoard Chart (p. 98). In addition it contained four relevant tetradrachms: one of Miletus with ΣΕ-bipennis (T. 246b), one of Sardes with ΜΗ-star (T. 386e) and two others with Ⓚ (T. 407, 408).

Larissa (*IGCH* 168). For the publication of this third ANS hoard, see T. Martin, "A Third-Century B.C. Hoard from Thessaly at the ANS," *ANSMN* 28 (forthcoming). Eight drachms of Miletus and 22 of Sardes are entered in the present catalogues and recorded by issues on the Hoard Chart (p. 98).

Bab (*IGCH* 1534). The hoard has been published with illustration but many of the coins are in such poor condition that precise die identifications are hazardous. Five of Miletus (T. 65, 96, 193b, 237b, 255) and three of Sardes (T. 80a, 105b, 124) are catalogue entries.

Susa (*IGCH* 1799). Ten drachms from this small hoard are illustrated by Le Rider but the only one from our mints (Sardes with ΔΕ-rose) is too worn for die comparison. There is also a Milesian drachm with Ⓐ -bipennis from c. 295 B.C. and a Magnesian issue with maeander in the exergue, which was probably struck shortly after the death of Lysimachus.

Olympia (*IGCH* 176). One Sardes drachm with ΔΕ-torch (T. 196d; N. 59).

Mesopotamia ante 1920 (*IGCH* 1764). From Sardes there are two late tetradrachms (T. 363, 381b) and three drachms of the time of Philip III (T. 214d, 346a, 347d).

Sparta (*IGCH* 181). On late tetradrachm of Sardes with ΜΗ-star (T. 380a).

Zemun (*IGCH* 458). A published hoard with very worn coins of Miletus and Sardes. One Milesian tetradrachm with ΣΕ-bipennis is in the present catalogue (T. 248c).

Corinth (*IGCH* 187). Again a published hoard from the end of the third century. Thompson and Noe numbers for catalogue entries are as follows:

Miletus: T. 78b, 233b, 247d = N. 183-84, 155

Sardes: T. 55, 140, 333c = N. 192-94

Mosul 1917 (*IGCH* 1768). Two drachms of Miletus (T. 39b, 265a) and three of Sardes (T. 271, 346b and c).

Published hoards from Gordion (*IGCH* 1401, 1403-6) and Euboea (*IGCH* 175, 205) have material from our mints. All are late third-century deposits with the fourth-century coins in poor condition. Die comparisons have not been attempted.

HOARD CHART

SARDES DRACHMS

	Asia Minor '64	*Sinan*	*Cavalla*	*Armenak**	*Larissa*
IV: Griffin's hd.	1				
VI: Bucranium	1			1	
VII: Cantharus		3			
VIII: Mithras hd.					
IX: [monogram]	1	21	3	2(8)	3
X: [monogram]	4	34	1	2(15)	3
XI: NK	1	12	3	3(3)	
XII: [monogram]		6		4(1)	1
XIII: [monogram]	2	29	2	7(3)	6
XIV: TI		65	13	8(15)	3
XV:: A		7	11	18(28)	5
XX: [monogram]			2	11(3)	1
	10	177	35	56(76)	22

MILETUS DRACHMS

	Asia Minor '64	*Sinan*	*Cavalla*	*Armenak**	*Larissa*
I: [monogram]	10	56	10	4(42)	2
III: Barley	1	1	2		
VII: [monogram]		15	1	1(1)	
VIII: [monogram]		1	1	6	1
IX: Crest			3	4(10)	1
X: [monogram]				2(3)	
XII: [monogram]				1	
XIII: [monogram]				2(1)	2
[monogram]			3	8(5)	2
	11	73	20	28(62)	8

* Numbers in parentheses indicate coins which Newell recorded but did not purchase.

PLATES

PLATE 1

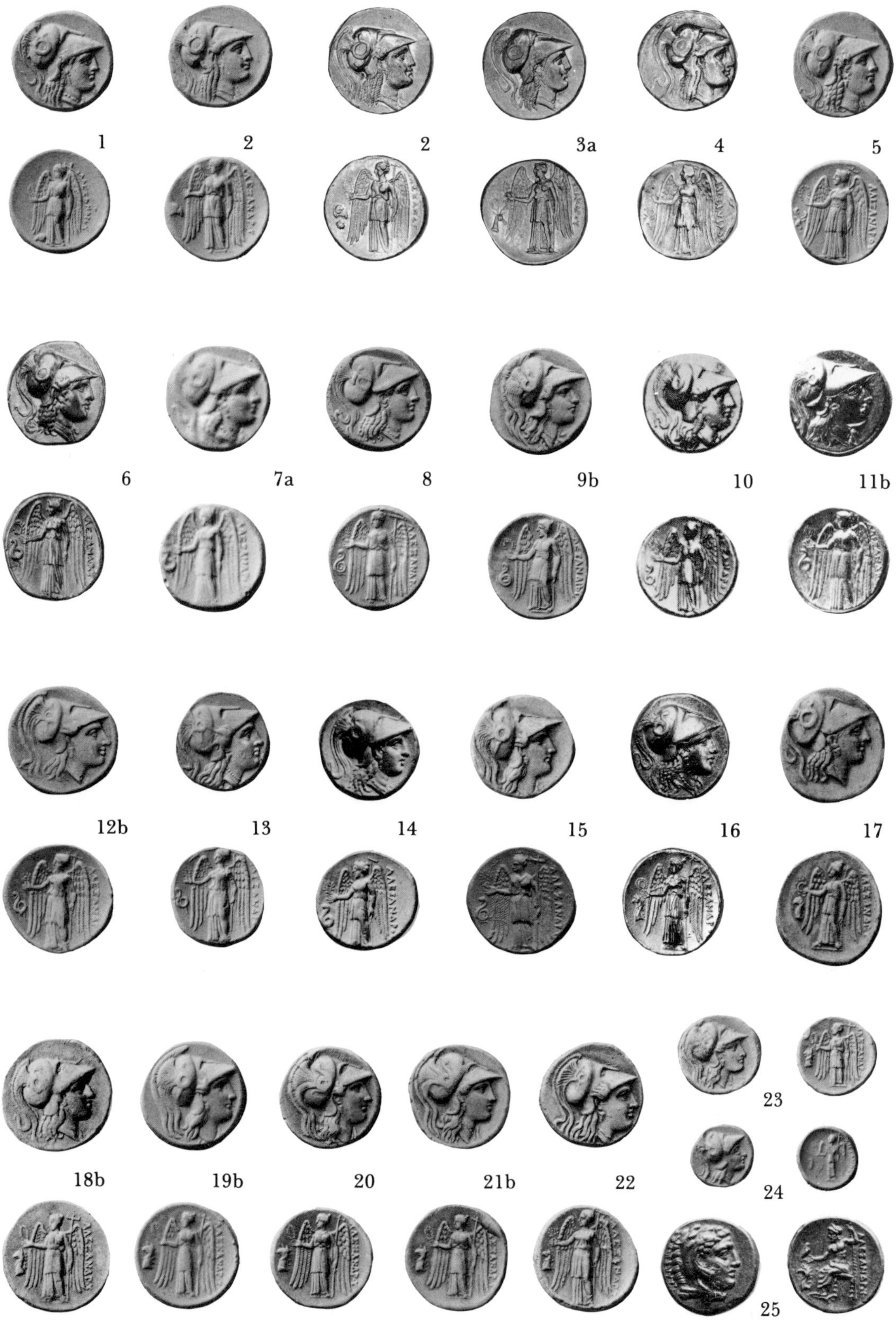

1 2 2 3a 4 5

6 7a 8 9b 10 11b

12b 13 14 15 16 17

18b 19b 20 21b 22 23 24 25

SARDES

PLATE 2

26 27a 28 29 30 31 32 33 34 35b 36 37a 39 38 40 41 42a 43 44 45 46 47 48 49 50 51

SARDES

PLATE 3

52 53 54a 54c

56a 57a 58a 59a 60a 61a

62 64 65a 66a 67a 68a

70 71 72 73 74 74a

SARDES

PLATE 4

75 76 77 78a 79a

80a 81 82 83a 84a

85a 87 88 89a 90a

91a 92 93 94 95

SARDES

PLATE 5

96a 96b 97 98 99 100

101 102 103 104 105a 106

107 109 110a 111a 112 113a

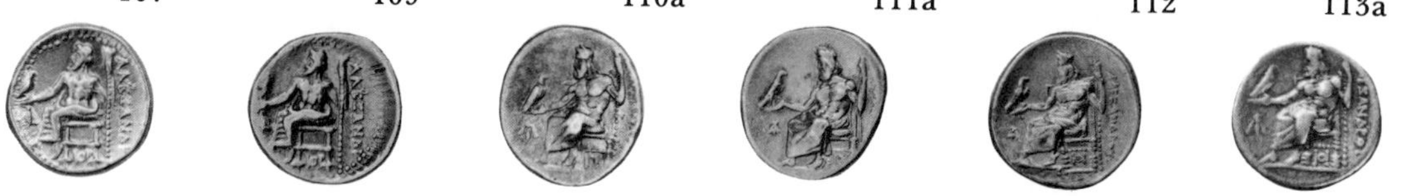

115 116a 117a 118a 119a 120

SARDES

PLATE 6

SARDES

PLATE 7

146a 146c 147 148 149a 150

151 152 153b 154a 155 156a

157 158b 159a 160 161 162

163a 164 165 166 167 168

SARDES

PLATE 8

169 170 171 172a 172c 173

174

175 176 178

179b 180 181 182a 183a 184a

185 186a 187 188a 189 190a

SARDES

PLATE 9

191 192b 194a 195 196a 197

199a 200 201b 202 203 204

205 207 208 209 210 211a

212 213 214a 215 216 217

SARDES

PLATE 10

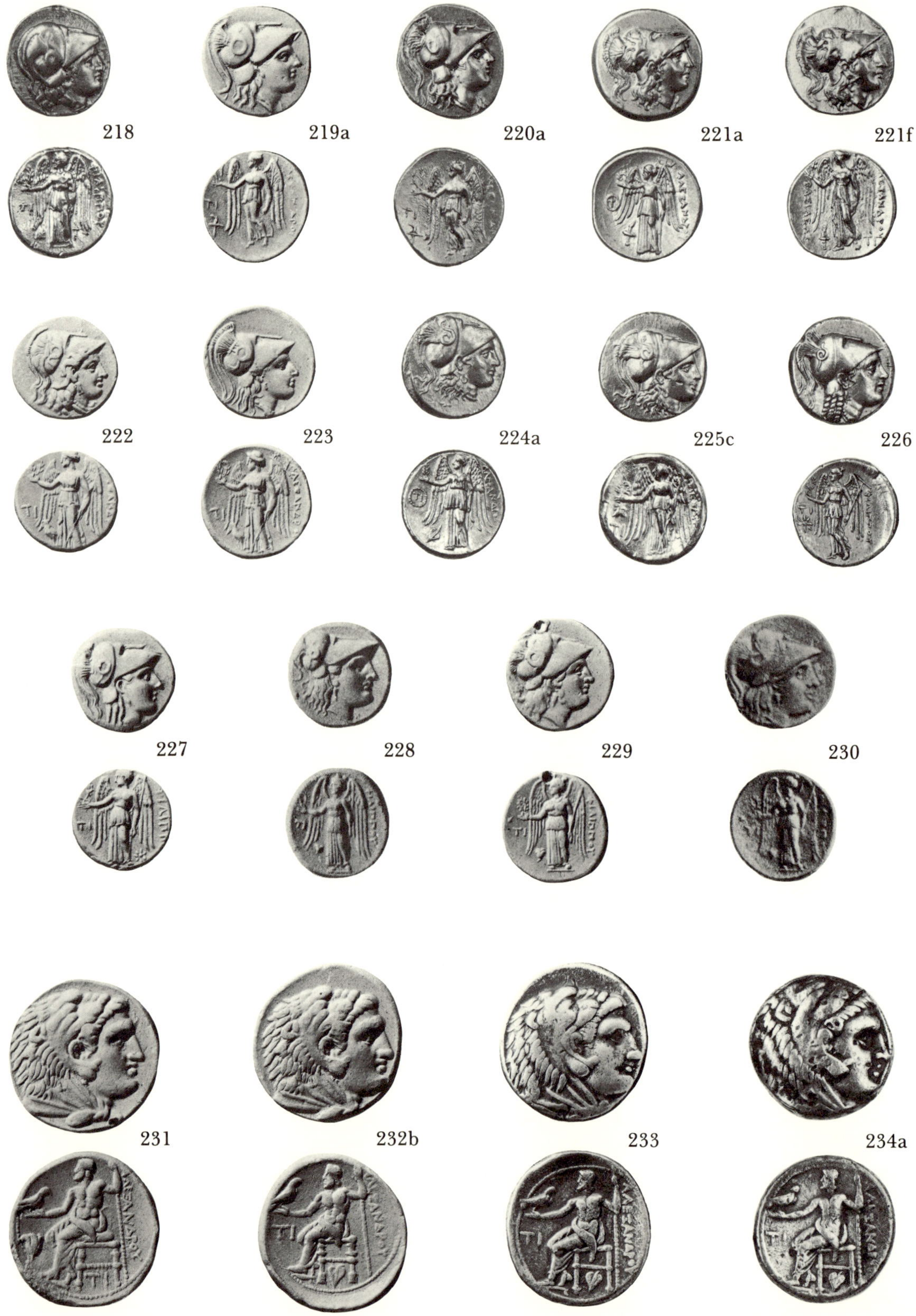

SARDES

PLATE 11

235a 236a 237a 238a

239g 240 241 242

243 243 244 245 246a 246c

247 248b 249 250 251 252

SARDES

PLATE 12

253b 254a 254b 255a 255b 256

257 258c 259a 260 261 262

263 264a 265 266 267 268

269 270 271 272a 273a 274

SARDES

PLATE 13

275 276c 277b 278a 279a 279d

280a 280d 281 282 283b 284b

285c 286a 287a 288a 289b 290a

291 292a 293c 294c 295 296

SARDES

PLATE 14

297 298 299 300a 301a 302

303a 303b 304

305a 305c 306 307

308a 308b 309 310

SARDES

311 312a 313a 314a 315 317a

318 319a 320a 320b 321a 322

323 324a 326 327 328 329

330 331 332 333a 334a 335

SARDES

PLATE 16

336a 337 338 339a 340 341

342 343a 344a 345a 345c 346b

347a 348 350a 351a 352a 353a

354a 355b 356a 356b 357a 357c

SARDES

PLATE 17

358

359

360

361

362

363

364

365a

366

367

368

369e

369g

370

SARDES

PLATE 18

371

372b

373

374

375

376a

377b

378

379a

379f

380a

380a

380c

381a

SARDES

PLATE 19

382d 383b 384a 385a 386a

387a 387b 387c 388 389 390a

391a 392 393 394e 395

SARDES

PLATE 20

396a 397b 398a 399 400b

401 402 403a 404 405a 406

407

408

409 410a 410c 411 412

SARDES

PLATE 21

1 2 3b 4 5 6b

7a 8a 9a 10 11 12a

13 14 15 16 17 18b

19c 20 21a

22 23

MILETUS

PLATE 22

MILETUS

PLATE 23

68b 72 73 74 76a 80

82a 84a 85 86b 89 90a

91a 92a 97 100a 101 103a

106a 109a 110b 111a 112 113a

MILETUS

PLATE 24

114 116a 118a 120 121 123

124a 124b

125 126 127a 128 129

130 131 132

133 134b 135 136a

MILETUS

PLATE 25

137a 137d 138

139a 140a 142 143 144 145

146

147

148a

149 151 152 155 156

MILETUS

PLATE 26

157

158b

159a

159e

160

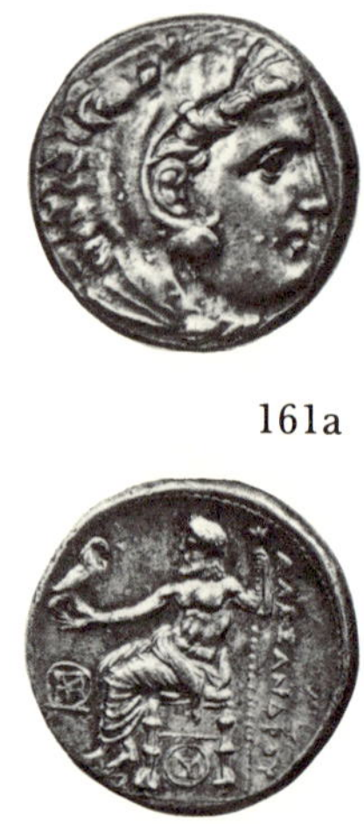

161a

162d

163c

164b

165a

166

167

168

MILETUS

169a 169b 170c 171b 172

173 174a 175a 176b 177

179 178 180

181g 182a 183b 184

MILETUS

PLATE 28

185b 186 187 188 189 190

191b 192 193a 194a 196 197

198 199 200 201 202

204 205 206

207

MILETUS

208 209 210 211a 212a 213a

214 215 216 217 218 219

220 221 222 223 224

225 226 227 228 229a 231a

MILETUS

PLATE 30

232a 233a 234 235 236 237a

238 239 240

241a

242 243 244

245 246c 247c 248c

MILETUS

PLATE 31

249a 250a 251 252a

253 254 256 257 258a A

259 260a 262b 263a 264b

265a 267 269 272 B C

MILETUS

PLATE 32

ASIA MINOR 1950

PLATE 33

JASNA POLJANA

PLATE 34

ASIA MINOR 1964

25 26 28 30 31 32

33 34 35 36 37 38

39 40 41 42 43 44

45 46 47 48 49 50

ASIA MINOR 1964

PLATE 36

51 52 53 54 55 56

57 58 59 60 62 63

64 65 66 67 68 69

71 72 73 74 75 76

ASIA MINOR 1964

ASIA MINOR 1964; NO. GREECE ANTE 1966

PLATE 38

SINAN PASHA